Praise

The post–B[...] [...]ng for a deeper, more meaningful way to engage in fomenting social change. Tired of always being against but never for, or the outsider who parachutes into a community in a time of crisis, we've been looking for other models to expand our praxis as anarchists and autonomists. Andrew Cornell's book is a thoughtful history of a group of thinkers and dreamers in the 1970s that grappled with similar questions. We Seattle babies can learn much from studying the experience of the previous generation.

—Yvonne Yen Liu, Colorlines.com

A thousand thanks to Andrew Cornell for resurrecting and analyzing the history of Movement for a New Society. Young organizers now won't have to reinvent the wheel—or the nonviolent antiauthoritarian collective. Especially insightful are the extended interviews with George Lakey and other MNS veterans. This book is the next best thing to having been there; maybe better, actually.

—Mark Rudd, author of *Underground: My Life in SDS and Weatherman*

This book is a gift. More than the biography of a twentieth-century organization, *Oppose and Propose!* is a set of practical tools for twenty-first-century organizers. In the interrogation of its history, Andrew Cornell takes the reader on a journey though the boom-and-bust cycles of Movement for a New Society, and thus illuminates the recurring challenges activists commonly face today. Reading this book was like watching the praxis wheel furiously spin, generating new questions and insights, helping us become students of our context. Cornell reminds us that we are indeed standing on the shoulders of our ancestors.

—Joshua Kahn Russell, Ruckus Society

OPPOSE AND PROPOSE!

LESSONS FROM MOVEMENT FOR A NEW SOCIETY

Anarchist Interventions | Two

Oppose and Propose! Lessons from Movement for a New Society
by Andrew Cornell

ISBN 978 1 849350 66 2 | Ebook: 978 1 849350 67 9
Library of Congress Number: 2011920473

© 2011 Andrew Cornell
This edition © 2011 AK Press and the Institute for Anarchist Studies
Cover Design and Interior: Josh MacPhee/Justseeds.org
Illustrations: Kristine Virsis/Justseeds.org

Printed in Canada on 100% recycled, acid-free paper by union labor

AK Press
674-A 23rd Street
Oakland, CA 94612
www.akpress.org
akpress@akpress.org
510.208.1700

AK Press U.K.
PO Box 12766
Edinburgh EH8 9YE
www.akuk.com
ak@akedin.demon.co.uk
0131.555.5165

Institute for Anarchist Studies
P.O. Box 15586
Washington, DC 20003
www.anarchist-studies.org
info@anarchiststudies.org

At least 50 percent of the net sales from each title in the Anarchist
Interventions series are donated to the IAS, thanks to the generosity
of each author.

OPPOSE AND PROPOSE!

LESSONS FROM MOVEMENT FOR A NEW SOCIETY

Andrew Cornell

AK Press / Institute for Anarchist Studies | 2011

Anarchist Interventions:

An IAS/AK Press Book Series

Radical ideas can open up spaces for radical actions, by illuminating hierarchical power relations and drawing out possibilities for liberatory social transformations. The Anarchist Intervention series—a collaborative project between the Institute for Anarchist Studies (IAS) and AK Press—strives to contribute to the development of relevant, vital anarchist theory and analysis by intervening in contemporary discussions. Works in this series will look at twenty-first-century social conditions—including social structures and oppression, their historical trajectories, and new forms of domination, to name a few—as well as reveal opportunities for different tomorrows premised on horizontal, egalitarian forms of self-organization.

Given that anarchism has become the dominant tendency within revolutionary milieus and movements today, it is crucial that anarchists explore current phenomena, strategies, and visions in a much more rigorous, serious manner. Each title in this series, then, will feature a present-day anarchist voice, with the aim, over time, of publishing a variety of perspectives. The series' multifaceted goals are to cultivate anarchist thought so as to better inform anarchist practice, encourage a culture of public intellectuals and constructive debate within anarchism, introduce new generations to anarchism, and offer insights into today's world and potentialities for a freer society.

Contents

Introduction

*O**ppose and Propose!* is about a now-defunct organization—Movement for a New Society (MNS)—that
I think people who struggle for justice and radical
political transformation should know more about. As the
title suggests, however, the book is also about the questions of political strategy, priorities, and tensions that MNS
grappled with, and that organizers continue to confront today. Among other issues, the history of MNS speaks to: the
role of "prefigurative" activities, confrontational organizing
campaigns, and direct action tactics in creating fundamental social change; the existence of a long-standing tradition
of anarchist pacifism and what it has to offer current movements; the organization question—that is, How should
we structure and coordinate our movements?; and ways of
proactively addressing race and class divisions, which often
undermine social movements in the United States. The history of MNS is fascinating and inspirational; most important, it's also instructional. MNS recognized that we have
to simultaneously *oppose* institutions, ways of life, social
relationships, and representations of groups of people that

are oppressive, exploitative, and alienating, while *proposing* (and beginning to create) new relations and institutions that promote dignity and a life lived in common. Members of the organization struggled mightily to do both of these things, and there is much we can learn from their achievements as well as their shortcomings.

Let me say a few words about how this book came about and what you will find between its covers. In 1998, I was fortunate to have a job at the Labadie Collection in Ann Arbor, Michigan, one of the largest archives of radical literature in the United States. One day I mentioned to Julie Herrada, the head archivist and perhaps the most knowledgeable person on the subject of anarchism I'd ever met, that my summer plans included a trip through Philadelphia. She replied, "You should check out West Philly. Anarchists own a bunch of property there." I thought she was testing me. "Yeah, right!" I shot back. "What happened to 'Property is theft'?" Julie tried to clarify: "Seriously—they own a bunch of cooperative houses and an anarchist community center. They own them *collectively*." I was intrigued and decided I needed to learn more about what sounded like a left-wing fairyland to my midwestern small-town ears.

Through a series of events, I ended up moving to West Philadelphia in summer 2001. And Julie was right. There were at least a dozen gigantic Victorian-style houses, with six or more radicals living in each, located within a ten-block radius. The homes were all served by a small neighborhood food co-op, and many of their residents frequented an anarchist community space a couple doors down. As

I got to know people involved in ACT-UP, Books through Bars, and other political work, I'd ask them, "Who started all this? Where did these houses come from?" Usually they'd shrug and say, "Movement for a New Society." When I pressed them for more information, they rarely had more details to share: "They were some group in the 1970s, I think."

Over the course of living in Philadelphia for a few years, I gathered additional bits of information here and there. MNS was a national network of radical pacifists that made West Philly their home base in the 1970s and 1980s. They had pooled their resources to buy houses, so they could live inexpensively and spend more time on their political work. They organized the food co-op and what is now called the A-Space had originally served as their office. The group had disbanded sometime in the 1980s, but some of the houses were still owned by a land trust that promoted cooperative living and cheap digs for organizers. In the late 1980s and throughout the 1990s, many of the younger radicals flocking to the neighborhood identified as anarchists. They organized campaigns to free political prisoners, established community gardens, organized punk shows, and began to squat additional houses, many of which were left vacant as white flight, deindustrialization, and other factors negatively affected the neighborhood. I found all this fascinating, but saw it mostly as a local phenomenon.

It wasn't until years later, when I began researching the history of anarchism in the United States after World War I, that I started to recognize how substantial an impact MNS had on the kind of political work, inside and outside anarchist circles, with which I'd long been involved. By reading old books and journals that MNS had published, and tracking down and talking with former members, I began to realize that they had been among the most outspoken and influential proponents of a whole litany of practices that seemed to define anarchist politics throughout the country in the late 1990s and 2000s: consensus decision making, large-scale direct action campaigns using affinity groups and spokescouncils, collective living in major cities, calling other activists out on their "shit," and much more. MNS did not consider itself an anarchist organization, but members readily admitted that anarchism was one major influence on their work. In turn, MNS has had a significant impact on contemporary anarchist politics, even though most anarchists I meet know next to nothing about the group. I realized, then, that the history of MNS would probably provide considerable insight for contemporary antiauthoritarian organizers and others seeking to reinvent a viable, vibrant politics and culture dedicated to overcoming war, racism, capitalism, and other forms of social domination.

In January 2008, the IAS awarded me a research grant to write an article about MNS. That article appears (in slightly modified form) as the first section of this book, "Movement for a New Society and Contemporary Anarchism." The article was published on the IAS Web site (http://www.anarchist-studies.org) in summer 2009, and the institute's journal, *Perspectives on Anarchist Theory*, in early 2010. I received a lot of positive feedback from former members of MNS and younger organizers who found that the article addressed tricky issues they were dealing with in their own political work. Since some readers were interested in communicating with former MNS members, George Lakey, who had helped found the group in 1971, suggested we organize public meetings where former MNS members and interested people could meet and discuss MNS's legacy. With help from a large crew, we held well-attended events in both New York City and Philadelphia. The enthusiasm and interest in learning about MNS shown by people attending those events encouraged me to develop this book in order to continue the conversation.

The second section of the book contains two pieces. The first is an interview with Lakey that Andrew Willis Garcés and I conducted when I was first researching MNS. The second is an edited transcript from the New York City and Philadelphia events, including short talks by five former MNS members as well as the question-and-answer sessions that followed. In both pieces, former MNS members describe the organization in their own words, adding important details and elaborating on themes I examine in my historical article. They also speak to challenges facing contemporary organizers, and draw connections and contrasts between the two periods.

The third section of the book is comprised of excerpts from two key MNS documents. The first, *Why Nonviolence?* was written after the historic Seabrook antinuclear power direct action campaign. MNS distributed over one hundred thousand copies of the article as a special newsprint edition of its newsletter, *Dandelion*. The essay does three things at once. First, it provides a brief overview of revolutionary nonviolence in the United States, indicating the crucial anarchist contributions to this tradition, which MNS saw itself as continuing. Second, it gives additional information about the Seabrook demonstrations, which constitute a significant chapter in the history of MNS as well as U.S. movements centered on direct action more generally. Finally, the article concisely articulates basic elements of nonviolent strategy that seem in danger of being forgotten by radicals today.

This section also includes brief excerpts from MNS's final *Organizational Handbook*, which outline the group's conclusions about the need for radical organizations, its vision of "shared leadership," and principles by which it attempted to practice self-management in its political work. These remarks will be pertinent to those on the left presently attempting to develop organizational forms that allow for effective, strategic, and coordinated national and international campaigns, while also trying to avoid re-creating disempowering, authoritarian, and class-divided institutions to carry out their own work.

In the conclusion, I draw out themes from each of the sections to indicate the relevance of MNS's thinking and activities for contemporary social justice work. Since this book comprises a contribution to the IAS/AK Press Anarchist Interventions series, I outline a variety of lessons and interventions that I believe the history of MNS makes in terms of present-day anarchist thinking and activity, relating these to an assortment of recent theoretical and strategic texts. I believe the history of MNS is relevant and will be of interest to a wide variety of people who do not identify as anarchists, however, and I hope this focus will not discourage anyone from exploring ideas contained herein.

Anarchism has historically meant many things to many people, and today is still too often used as a term of dismissal or abuse. I, personally, am most attracted to a conceptualization of the idea recently offered by the North American Anarchist Studies Network: "We understand anarchism, in general terms, as the practice of equality and freedom in every sphere of life—life conceived and lived without domination in any form; we understand this practice to belong not only to a better future but to the here and now, where we strive to prefigure our ends in the means we choose to reach them."[1]

Anarchism, then, serves as an ethical compass for action in daily life, and a vision of a participatory democratic social order that progressive social movements should continuously strive to develop and move others toward, whether or not it can ever be reached in absolute terms. There seems to be a growing consensus among those on the Left, whether they call themselves anarchists, decentralized socialists, participatory and radical democrats, Zapatistas, or small "c" communists, that neither authoritarian socialist nor liberal democratic state forms allow for the possibility of generalizing human dignity and equality on a world scale. The honest search for political forms that do hold out such potential is what I am most invested in and was, I believe, at the heart of MNS's political project as well.

Oppose and Propose! is meant as one step in the process of recovering and sharing the history as well as the ideas of MNS. I hope that someone will soon write a comprehensive history of MNS and the milieu it operated within, but this is not that book. Rather than a history, an organizational biography, or a hagiography, this book might best be thought of as an experiment in militant coresearch. By this I mean that it is research conducted by, with, and for radicals with the express purpose of gaining insights that concretely facilitate current and future movement activities. The book is a record of ongoing inquiries and conversations as well as an invitation for you to participate in them. It's my hope that the material presented here will inspire our movements to collectively seek innovative solutions to the organizing challenges we face, so that we might more powerfully oppose the degrading values and institutions that structure our daily lives, and more brilliantly propose humane and sustainable replacements for them.

Acknowledgments

This book wouldn't have been possible without the contributions of a large number of people. From the get-go it has been a collective endeavor. First and foremost this includes the former MNS members whose voices comprise nearly half the book: Bob Irwin, George Lakey, Betsy Raasch-Gilman, Nancy Brigham, and Lynne Shivers. I especially want to thank Bob for taking the time to read through the entire manuscript and serving as a sounding board throughout the process. Kristine Virsis and Josh MacPhee of the Justseeds Artists' Cooperative made the book beautiful with their incredible illustrations and design skills, respectively. The title of the book derives from a panel that

Dara Greenwald and Denisse Andrade organized at the Left Forum conference in 2009. They generously allowed me to borrow their useful formulation of "the oppositional and the propositional." I have been encouraged and supported throughout the project by the IAS. I especially want to thank Cindy Milstein, Joshua Stephens, Chris Dixon, and Harjit Singh Gill, who encouraged me to write the book, and then served as capable editors and advisers as I developed the project. Zach Blue, Charles Weigl, and Kate Khatib at AK Press were encouraging, flexible, helpful, and friendly.

Ronnie Almonte and Pat Korte of the Organization for a Free Society, along with Kazembe Balagun and Max Uhlenbeck of the Brecht Forum, helped organize the New York City MNS event. In Philadelphia, Kristin Campbell, Alex Knight, Jeremy Ross, Sarah Small, Ivan Booth, Scott Campbell, and Erik Ruin organized an amazing event. The Prometheus Radio Project and Studio 34 made crucial donations of space and equipment. My sister, Kerstin Cornell, quickly transcribed hours of audiotape from the events. I also want to thank former MNS member Jay Shefsky, who shared photographs of the organization, which appeared in *Perspectives on Anarchist Theory* alongside my article. Due to an oversight, he was not credited for his excellent photos. I offer both my gratitude and apologies here. I want to offer a special thanks to my close friend and comrade, Dan Berger, for all the political smarts and book publishing advice that he has shared with me. Finally, I offer my love and gratitude to my partner, the ever-brilliant, talented, and supportive Jessica Harbaugh.

HISTORY

Movement for a New Society and Contemporary Anarchism

The international anarchist movement found new footings in the wake of the global insurrections of 1968, nearly all of which were decidedly libertarian in character.[1] In the United States, the decade that followed was a time of experimentation and consolidation, as a surprising variety of groups sought to develop and adapt different aspects of the anarchist tradition to contemporary conditions. Sam Dolgoff and others worked to revitalize the Industrial Workers of the World (IWW) alongside new syndicalist formations like the Chicago-based Resurgence group and Boston's Root and Branch. Murray Bookchin's *Anarchos* journal collective deepened the theoretical links between ecological and anarchist thought. The *Fifth Estate* magazine drew heavily on French ultraleftist thinking and began pursuing a critique of technology by the decade's end. Meanwhile, the Social Revolutionary Anarchist Federation connected individuals and circles across the country through a mimeographed monthly discussion bulletin. Just as influential to the anarchist milieu that has taken shape in the decades that have followed, however, were the efforts of Movement for a New Society (MNS), a national network of feminist, radical pacifist collectives that existed from 1971 to 1988.[2]

Though MNS is rarely remembered by name today, its many new ways of doing radical politics have become central to contemporary antiauthoritarian social movements. MNS popularized consensus decision making, introduced the spokescouncil method of organization to radicals in the United States, and was a leading advocate of a variety of practices—such as communal living, unlearning oppressive behavior, and creating cooperatively owned businesses— that are now often subsumed under the rubric of prefigurative politics.[3] MNS was significantly shaped by aspects of anarchist thought and practice developed both in the United States and abroad. Participants synthesized these elements with an array of others to develop an experimental revolutionary practice that attempted to combine multi-issue political analysis, organizing campaigns, and direct action with the creation of alternative institutions, community building, and personal transformation.[4] Although MNS never claimed more than three hundred members, it bore an influence on 1970s' radicalism disproportionate to its size, owing to both the strategy and skills trainings in which the group specialized, and the ways in which MNS's vision overlapped with significant developments in the broader feminist and environmental movements.

As antiauthoritarians have widely adopted practices and

perspectives that MNS promoted, some—such as the use of consensus process and a focus on establishing new ways of living—have become so hegemonic within movement culture that they are frequently taken as transhistorical tenets of anarchist politics or radicalism more generally. A lack of critical historical evaluation has, unfortunately, led many groups to adopt basic elements that MNS tried out, without also taking up the important lessons that participants derived from the shortcomings of their political experiments. A brief exploration of MNS's history, then, may offer insights into dilemmas faced by our contemporary movements.

Radical Pacifism and Anarchism

MNS grew out of a Quaker antiwar organization in 1971, but it built on traditions that radical pacifists had developed throughout the twentieth century. After World War I, a new form of pacifist movement developed in the United States that was socialist and based on secular, rather than religious, rationales for opposing violence. While a commitment to ending all forms of war remained the movement's primary focus, participants recognized that this required them to oppose the underlying causes of war—namely, capitalism and the imperialism it spurred. Pacifists distinguished their methods from those of the major leftist parties by insisting on a correlation between means and ends, and encouraging adherents to live in a fashion as similar as possible to the ways they would in the ideal society they were striving for.[5]

By the onset of World War II, this radical pacifist movement had incorporated a variety of crucial anarchist influences. Gandhian philosophy, which became the movement's primary inspiration, was of course heavily influenced by Henry David Thoreau's individualism and Leo Tolstoy's Christian anarchism. Yet Dutch anarcho-pacifist Bart de Ligt's 1936 treatise *The Conquest of Violence* (with its none-too-subtle allusion to Peter Kropotkin's *The Conquest of Bread*) was also of signal importance.[6] These thinkers deepened the pacifist critique of war to question forms of institutional social violence, and highlighted the contradiction between the state's "monopoly on legitimate violence" and pacifist tenets. Domestically, radical pacifist circles overlapped considerably with those of a small cohort of anarchists in the 1940s, including figures such as Ammon Hennacy, Paul Goodman, and Audrey Goodfriend. Young male anarchists such as David Wieck, Cliff Bennett, and Lowell Naeve resisted conscription during World War II, and found themselves imprisoned with Gandhian pacifists such as David Dellinger and Bill Sutherland. These war resisters protested segregation and other conditions in the federal penitentiaries through noncooperation, influencing one another's politics in the process. Anarchists of this period departed from previous generations not only by embracing pacifism but also by devoting more energy to promoting avant-garde culture, preparing the ground for the beat generation in the process.[7] The editors of the anarchist journal *Retort*, for instance, produced a volume of writings by draft resisters imprisoned in Danbury, Connecticut, while regularly publishing the poetry and prose of writers such as Kenneth Rexroth and Norman Mailer. From the 1940s to the 1960s, the radical pacifist movement in the United States thus harbored both social democrats and anarchists, at a time when the anarchist movement itself seemed on its last legs. During these years, pacifists formed organizations such as the Committee for Nonviolent Revolution and Peacemakers, which experimented with network structures and consensus decision-making processes.[8] A pacifist wing has existed alongside other anarchist tendencies in the United States ever since. The concerns and approach adopted by MNS derive in large measure from the different itineraries taken by members of this earlier radical milieu during the 1960s.

Radical pacifists created the Congress of Racial Equality in 1942, and were important conduits of participatory deliberative styles and the tactics of Gandhian nonviolence to leaders of the civil rights movement, including Martin Luther King Jr. and members of the Student Nonviolent Coordinating Committee (SNCC).[9] Meanwhile, the beat culture, incubated by anarchists in the 1940s, fed into the more explicitly political counterculture of the 1960s. Students for a Democratic Society (SDS) drew on SNCC's participatory structure and the ethos of the counterculture to formulate two of the defining demands of the New Left: the implementation of participatory democracy, and the dissolution of alienating culture.[10] Yet in the later 1960s, both the black freedom and student movements, smarting from repression, on the one hand, and elated by radical victories at home and abroad, on the other, moved away from this emergent, anarchistic, political space distinguished from both liberalism and Marxism. Many civil rights organizers took up nationalist politics in hierarchical organizations, while some of the most committed SDS members turned to variants of Marxist-Leninism and democratic socialism.[11]

If participatory democracy and cultural transformation could, together, be seen as a ball about to be dropped, MNS was one of the most important groups diving for it, working hard to keep it in play. The emergent women's liberation movement likewise placed a premium on developing egalitarian internal relationships and making changes in daily life; not surprisingly, feminism also left an enduring impact on MNS.[12]

MNS emerged in 1971 as the new face of A Quaker Action Group (AQAG), a Philadelphia-based direct action group that had carried out creative "witnesses" against the devastation of the Vietnam War, hoping to "undermine the legitimacy of the [U.S.] government."[13] Perhaps most famously, members piloted a fifty-foot ship, the *Phoenix*, on three trips to North and South Vietnam in 1967 and 1968 with cargoes of donated medical supplies.[14] By 1969, however, AQAG leaders began to recognize that the movement should aim not only to end the war in Vietnam but also to fundamentally reshape all aspects of U.S. life. AQAG presented a proposal to the American Friends Service Committee (AFSC) in March 1971, arguing that the times—and Quaker principles—called for a broad program to combat ecological devastation, militarism, "corporate capitalism," racism, and sexism. The statement succinctly laid out a new vision for creating "fundamental change":

We hope to catalyze a movement for a new society, which will feature a vision of the new society, and how to get there; a critical analysis of the American political-economic system; a focus on expanding the consciousness and organizing the commitment of the middle class toward fundamental change through nonviolent struggle, often in concert with other change movements; the organization and development of nonviolent revolutionary groups and life centers as bases for sustained struggle on the local as well as national and international levels; training for non-violent struggle; and a program rooted in changed lives and changed values.[15]

Although some members expressed considerable sympathy for the proposal, the AFSC declined to adopt it. Undeterred, the coterie of approximately two-dozen radicals continued to meet, renaming themselves MNS to reflect the broader aims and secular status of their new initiative. Beginning with small collectives in Philadelphia and Eugene, Oregon, they set to work building membership and developing a program.

Analysis, Action, Community, and Training

Even though it was not officially sanctioned by the AFSC, MNS was able to draw on the support of an established network of Quaker institutions to enlist a critical mass of members in the new organization. This broader network

helped ensure the group's legitimacy, spread information, and provided monetary support crucial to attract-
ing enough participants early on. Nevertheless, reliance on
such a network for recruiting also contributed to the predominantly white and middle-class character of the organization's membership in its early years.[16]

MNS founders also undertook recruiting tours that
presented the group's approach as an alternative to the
style and pace of 1960s' movement work, which had taken
a significant personal toll in the form of widespread burn-
out by the early 1970s. Returning from one such trip,
Berit Lakey and Paul Morrissey reported that "people were
so varied—old people looking for new hope and young
people trying not to become cynical. . . . The wholeness of
the MNS approach—from analysis to action to community—generated excitement. More and more people are
questioning the value of their scattered activities. Fewer
and fewer are willing to put off their personal growth until
'after the revolution.'"[17]

Analysis

MNS's multi-issue, multisided approach to radical
change was first developed through a study group and collective writing project among AQAG leaders that resulted
in two books, which then served as the primary statements of MNS's politics: *Moving toward a New Society*
and *Strategy for a Living Revolution*.[18] As the organization took shape, the founders expanded the process of
collective political education and analysis to include any
member who was interested by developing "macroanalysis

seminars"—long-term collaborative study groups modeled after the popular education initiatives of the civil rights movement and the ideas of Paulo Freire.[19] MNS's focus on an overarching analysis that sought to link seemingly disparate social problems and forms of inequality was innovative for a period in which theorists fought to assert the primacy of racial, gender, or class oppression, and the concept of "intersectionality" was not yet widely accepted.[20]

Revolutionary nonviolence formed the bedrock of MNS's political analysis and strategy. The group believed that war is inherent to capitalism and social inequality is itself a form of violence, maintained by the threat of direct state violence; this requires those who morally reject violence to become social revolutionaries. Members synthesized these core principles with recent developments in leftist thought. Foremost, this entailed a commitment to the principles of ecology and environmental sustainability emerging at the time. MNS, additionally, placed the United States's neocolonial relationship with the countries of the global South at the center of its indictment of contemporary society. The group insisted on the need to "de-develop" the United States and other capitalist countries, as the members of these nations lived at consumption rates unattainable for the majority of the world's population and unsustainable given ecological limits.[21] Influenced by the nascent women's liberation movement, MNS incorporated from the outset a critique of sexism alongside its indictment of racism (shaped by some members' work in the civil rights movement). Yet white supremacy and patriarchy were given considerably less extensive treatment than political-economic concerns in the group's early publications and statements.[22] Bringing together a mix of Gandhians, anarchists, and unaffiliated democratic socialists, MNS promoted the idea of a "decentralized socialism" that had much in common with the "participatory economics" others were developing at the time.[23]

> Economic enterprises, as we see it, would be socially owned, decentralized and democratically controlled. . . . Political decisions would be made by participatory means, starting with the smallest face-to-face communities of citizens and extending upward to the global level. Nation-states as we now know them would cease to exist, supplanted by regional groupings, perhaps of those with common economic interests.[24]

MNS members were significantly influenced by a variety of anarchist titles published in the 1970s. Bookchin's 1971 *Post-Scarcity Anarchism* was a mainstay of the group's macroanalysis seminars, not only for its ecological arguments, but also for the history of alternative forms of radical organizing described in the essay "Listen, Marxist!" Seminar participants also read selections from the Black Rose volume *The Case for Participatory Democracy*, edited by Dimitri Roussopoulos, early works on libertarian socialism by Michael Albert and Robin Hahnel, and even selections from Alexander Berkman and Kropotkin. The discovery of Dolgoff's *The Anarchist Collectives*, a history of worker self-management during the Spanish Civil War, was important to MNS members' ability to imagine a process by which its collectives might develop into an entire social system.[25]

Still, many members were unaware of the influence of anarchist ideas on their organization, as attested to by a paper circulated internally in 1976, in which Bob Irwin, a member of the Philadelphia Macroanalysis Collective, argued that "the time has come to make explicit and evaluate the organization theory by which we have been operating.... That organization theory, I contend, is anarchism."[26] Although some members individually identified as anarchists, MNS never did so as an organization, and it doesn't appear to have had direct ties with any of the self-identified anarchist organizations of the 1970s. In its early years, MNS was sympathetic toward socialist initiatives such as the New American Movement and the Democratic Socialist Organizing Committee. Yet MNS hewed toward anarchist strategy by expressing "grave reservations" about electoralism or the potential for reradicalizing the labor movement in the United States.[27] The group believed that it could best contribute to the goal of establishing a self-managed economy by creating worker-owned cooperatives and other alternative institutions while working to foment a broad nonviolent insurrection, organized on the basis of directly democratic councils, capable of toppling the current political-economic order.

Anarchism was perhaps most influential on the organization's structure. MNS saw that in starting fresh, it had the chance to incorporate in its structure the principle—expressed most recently by the New Left, but earlier by anarchists and radical pacifists—that the movement should prefigure, or anticipate and model, its goals in its own work. MNS's introductory pamphlet declared its opposition to "traditional forms of organization, from [the multinational corporation] ITT to the PTA [Parent-Teacher Association] . . . for they exhibit the sexism and authoritarianism we seek to supplant. Our goals must be incorporated into the way we organize. Thus the movement we build must be egalitarian and non-centralized."[28] Accordingly, the group developed a network structure that was directly influenced by a Dutch anarchist federation, Shalom, which had impressed founding member George Lakey during his travels across Europe in 1969.[29]

From the outset, MNS members relied on a consensus decision-making process and rejected the domineering forms of leadership prevalent in 1960s' radical groups. The impetus to change the internal dynamics of radical organizations stemmed from a variety of sources. Inspired by SNCC—which in turn, had been influenced by pacifists such as James Lawson and Bayard Rustin—SDS had promoted the demand for a participatory form of democracy, but had never formalized the concept into a procedure. The early women's liberation movement responded to the sexism that marred New Left groups by roundly criticizing patriarchal leadership tendencies and attempting to craft egalitarian organizations of its own. The MNS founders sought to build on both these initiatives by developing and teaching a formal model of "democratic group process" that drew on the Quaker tradition in which many were steeped as well as the conflict resolution techniques that some early MNS members practiced as professional mediators.[30] Beyond adopting a formal consensus procedure with delineated roles, MNS drew on "sensitivity training" techniques, "role playing . . . listening exercises, and trust games" to increase awareness of group dynamics and challenge members to excise oppressive aspects of their traditional patterns of behavior.[31] Members saw at least three benefits to this process: it helped empower more reserved and less experienced participants; it kept in check the sometimes-competing egos of movement veterans involved in the organization; and finally, the highly deliberative aspect of consensus was useful in the group's early stage when it was "searching" for new ideas and building unity among its members.[32]

MNS's commitment to prefiguration was most frequently expressed in its injunction to "live the revolution now"—a reformulation of Mahatma Gandhi's classic instruction for his followers to "be the change you want to see." In its early statements, however, MNS was clear that "living the revolution" served as only one practical aspect of a multipronged revolutionary strategy, not an end in itself. "We need to simplify and organize our life together so there is time for the confrontations that are needed if the old order is to fall," begins the "Community" section of the group's introductory pamphlet. Like many other radical theorists in the early 1970s, the MNS founders believed that structural contradictions would create a crisis situation in the United States by the end of the century, if not the end of the decade.[33] Whether that crisis could be turned to revolutionary ends, though, would depend on the consciousness of the majority of the U.S. population.

MNS members believed they could serve as a "leaven in the bread" of the mass social movements responding to this crisis, giving them the tools and nonviolent principles they would need to effectively make a social revolution.[34] In the short term, they believed, radicals needed to develop strategic campaigns that combined organizing and direct action to win "revolutionary reforms" while simultaneously building alternative institutions based on radical principles, which could serve to model the future society.[35] For these efforts to be sustained throughout a long struggle and to ultimately be successful, organizers needed training and to experience new kinds of community supportive of their work.

Action

MNS demonstrated its approach to activism almost immediately. In July 1971, the newly minted group launched itself into the Baltimore harbor in a fleet of canoes and kayaks to blockade a Pakistani ship from docking to take on a shipment of military supplies. The confrontation grew out of a "study-action team" that began researching the impact of U.S. policies and business ties abroad. The team decided to focus on the Nixon administration's financial and military support for the Pakistani military dictatorship, known for its brutal suppression of political opponents and the people of East Pakistan (now Bangladesh). Though its first attempt at blocking a weapons shipment was defeated by police and Coast Guard officers, who hauled the peace fleet out of the water and into jail cells, the action received wide coverage in national print, radio, and television reportage.[36]

Neither discouraged nor satisfied with their results, MNS expanded the campaign. The group joined forces with the Philadelphia Friends of East Bengal, whose members were more directly impacted by the crisis in the subcontinent, and appealed to the International Longshoremen's Association, convincing the union to refuse to load military material bound for Pakistan. When MNS and its allies discovered another Pakistani ship was to take on supplies in Philadelphia in August, they again mobilized a sea blockade, but this time paired it with a picket on the docks. After an intense effort by the MNS fleet to evade police boats and place itself in the freighter's path, the *Al-Ahmadi* managed to dock. Still, following the lead of their local union president, the longshoremen refused to cross a picket line that MNS maintained continuously until the ship sailed away empty twenty-eight hours later.[37]

MNS deployed similar tactics in April 1972, when it allied with Vietnam Veterans against the War and local Quaker groups to block the *USS Nitro* from loading munitions bound for the Gulf of Tonkin. Though ultimately unsuccessful in blocking the ship, the skirmishes on land and sea proved so inspiring to the *Nitro*'s reluctant crew that five sailors literally jumped from the ship and attempted to join the war resisters in their canoes.[38]

These actions grew out of campaign models taught by MNS members with extensive experience in the civil rights and antiwar movements, including Bill Moyer and Richard Taylor, both of whom had held staff positions in the Southern Christian Leadership Conference, the organization led by King. The blockades reconfirmed the MNS strategists' belief that direct action could yield tangible results and educate the public through media coverage, but needed to be rooted in organizing campaigns and coalition building to be effective.[39]

If the port blockades demonstrated the commitment of Philadelphia MNS members to well-planned action, other developments showcased MNS as a national organization that was able to mobilize in solidarity with radical struggles on a moment's notice. When federal officials seemed poised to violently oust American Indian Movement members occupying the hamlet of Wounded Knee in March of 1973, MNS implemented a phone tree to contact participants throughout the network. Collectives in Madison, Minneapolis, Milwaukee, Des Moines, Denver, Portland, and Philadelphia responded by organizing carloads of people to converge on Wounded Knee within two days. On arrival, MNS members organized "observer teams" to position themselves between the troops and occupiers. Although the members may have forestalled violence in the first days, the government eventually forced their withdrawal.[40] MNS later launched nationally coordinated protests less than twenty-four hours after news broke of the Three Mile Island nuclear disaster in 1979.[41]

Community

Beginning with its first collective statement, MNS emphasized that a major component of its program would be the creation of intentional communities of activists. As first conceived, the movement would be made up of six-to-twelve person Nonviolent Revolutionary Groups (NRGs, or "Energies") that would work on issues as teams and "share their lives as well as work, sometimes living communally."[42] In *Strategy for a Living Revolution*, published in 1973, Lakey explicitly described NRGs as a contemporary form of affinity group, though he did not cite the anarchist origins of that organizational form.[43] MNS's founding document explained, "Through NRGs, individuals can seek to live the revolution now by giving up the characteristic scatter of liberal activities which results in fragmented selves and soulless organizations, and substitute concentration and community." MNS, then, was conceptualized as a "network of small groups rather than of individual members" that would coordinate their activities on the local, regional, and national levels. In areas where numerous groups were clustered, the movement would develop Life Centers: "more sizable, collective living arrangements for ongoing training and direct action campaigns."[44]

Members organized collective living situations in cities such as Savannah and Seattle, and smaller towns like Ann Arbor and Madison. Participants typically lived in communal households, and participated in one or more collectives focused on an aspect of the work (such as direct actions, trainings, or macroanalysis seminars). Citywide meetings and informal social gatherings knit the collectives together. Members dispersed geographically and involved in an expanding array of campaigns shared their ideas and experiences with one another through a lively internal newsletter, variously titled *Dandelion Wine*, *Wine*, and *Grapevine*, published monthly by an internal communications collective that rotated between MNS groups in different cities each year. The entire network met for a week, once a year, at Whole Network Meetings to socialize, strategize, and hash out policies affecting the entire organization. Whole Network Meetings in the mid-1970s brought together 100 to 120 people, usually about half of those participating in the organization in a given year.[45] The NRG terminology fell out of use after the first year, because rather than finding a primary political home in one specific affinity group, members tended to participate in multiple collectives as well as their households and the local MNS community; commitment to the network had trumped commitment to the individual NRG.

While many cities hoped to develop Life Centers, only Philadelphia was able to maintain a community large and stable enough to offer the number of activities, collectives, and alternative institutions originally envisioned. In January 1976, when an internal census was completed, a ten-block area of West Philadelphia was home to nineteen collective households composed of four to eleven people each, with names such as "The Gathering," "Kool Rock Amazons," and "Sunflower." Members of these households worked in twenty-two different MNS collectives, including the Feminist Collective, the Training Organizing Collective, the Simple Living Group, and the Peace Conversion/B-1 Bomber Collective.[46] Households operated independently—choosing their own members, and establishing policies about what was purchased jointly and how much members were required to contribute to expenses. Household cultures varied: some collectives shared religious practices, and others shared their entire incomes.[47] Until the mid-1980s, MNS did not pay anyone for movement work. Members were encouraged to work part-time jobs to earn the "bread money" they needed for monthly household expenses and personal items. Some members worked retail jobs, sometimes at cooperative enterprises, while others took on construction work, taught college courses, or staffed Quaker-related organizations.

MNS strategy prioritized the creation of alternative institutions that modeled egalitarian and anticapitalist values. Philadelphia members created a worker-owned print shop and a member-run food cooperative, while a Baltimore collective opened a toy store. Later, the MNS publications committee launched a commercial press, called New Society Publishers. These businesses provided jobs to MNS members along with services to the movement and others in the neighborhood. After a series of rapes, members also helped organize a block association that worked to prevent crime through community building. The block association rejected an increased police presence in favor of teams of neighbors that patrolled on foot, armed only with air horns. The association also offered victim counseling, which it believed was "helpful to prevent over-reaction in the longer run," meaning the racism underlying the crime fears of white people living in racially mixed areas of West Philadelphia.[48] Alternative institutions were meant to demonstrate that radical activity could create immediate, concrete improvements in people's daily lives—improvements, the founders believed, that would give organizers confidence, and were more likely than its seemingly remote utopian visions to attract neighbors and those not already radicalized to participate in MNS.[49]

Beyond serving as a base for alternative institutions, collective living was meant to allow members to live "simply" and inexpensively, permitting them to dedicate more time to movement work and reduce their environmental impact. Moreover, living in community was expected to promote the "personal growth" of MNS members. This commitment to individual transformation was perhaps the most ambiguous aspect of the MNS project, as it combined personal empowerment exercises with spirituality and the unlearning of oppressive behavior through a variety of radical therapy practices emergent at the time. Initially, members' commitment to personal growth meant involvement in self-help and self-care activities, such as yoga or learning to become "active listeners"—activities intended to aid them in becoming more effective in their daily lives and organizing work. Within the organization's first year, MNS members in Philadelphia began an extended process of understanding and rooting out sexism—and later homophobia, classism, and racism—within the organization as well as in members' personal lives.

As these discussions progressed, personal growth came to mean shedding the internalized strictures of an unjust society—racist and ageist conditioning, patriarchal gender roles, and bourgeois "hang-ups." Though this process started with discussions internal to the group, it grew to take on other forms, including the development of "theory papers" and educational work. A Philadelphia men's group, for instance, took steps to publicly challenge traditional gender roles by holding street meetings. Recounting an early experience, the group asked *Dandelion* readers to "imagine twenty men, speaking very personally about men's liberation, holding hands and hugging, giving each other the needed support for such a scary situation, singing loudly and proudly about how we don't want society's 'John Wayne Image.'"[50] MNS understood that the personal was political, and therefore, saw the process of individuals developing aspects of their personality not sanctioned or encouraged by social expectations as a victory in itself. They also understood that unlearning oppressive assumptions and behavior was crucial to becoming better organizers.

Complicating each of these aspects of personal growth was the penchant most MNS members shared for "radical therapy" practices such as transactional analysis and especially reevaluation counseling (RC, also known as "cocounseling").[51] Invented by former Communist Party member Harvey Jackins, RC seeks to overcome oppression through reciprocal psychological counseling sessions among nonprofessional individuals trained in the process. The theory proposes that all people have been oppressed, and suggests that the path to overcoming that oppression is through emoting about individual painful and shameful experiences, including those from childhood, in order for the cocounselor to move past emotional "blockages" and think in a fully rational manner. Jackins believed that after dissolving all such blockages, practitioners could inhabit a childlike state of joy and innocence.

Despite the therapy movement's hierarchical structure and revelations that Jackins had engaged in a pattern of sexual improprieties with female cocounselors, RC language and practice came to pervade MNS's work. When deliberating about sensitive issues, for example, members might remind each other that it was alright to act "on our feelings," but unhelpful to "act on our distress as it blurs good thinking."[52] In difficult meetings, facilitators often called for breaks to allow members to pair up for brief counseling sessions. In MNS, then, the Gandhian dictum that the revolutionaries must change as they change society merged with the growing interest in popular psychology, new age spirituality, and gurus that occupied many former radicals in the 1970s.[53] If the focus on personal development didn't depoliticize MNS members, as it did to many of their contemporaries, it did shift MNS work in an individualistic direction that would have serious consequences for the organization in years to come.

Beyond developing personal skills, MNS communities were intended to shape movement culture by changing how participants interacted with each other. In an attempt to correct for the harsh style of many 1960s' initiatives, MNS sought to model a form of radical politics that shunned aggressive and egoist behavior, and included emotional support for one's comrades as central to the mission of social change organizations. This culture of support manifested itself in many ways: the practice of physical affection, both platonic and romantic, through hugging and snuggling (nonmonogamy was widespread among members); collective singing and other forms of self-entertainment in the collective homes; and the habit of engaging in "light and livelies"—seemingly childish games (similar to today's icebreakers) to keep energy and spirits up during long meetings.

MNS, in summary, saw its form of collective living as an extension of the work undertaken in consciousness-raising groups and central to realizing the democratic ideal of individuals developing themselves to their greatest potential. A 1974 *Dandelion* article titled "MNS Support Communities" explained it this way:

> As members of the community gradually free themselves from oppressive roles and patterns of relating to each other (i.e., from sexist, ageist or racist conditioning), they provide an atmosphere of greater equality and openness for others. New members joining the community find themselves in an increasingly creative environment where they are being "asked"—simply by interacting with others—to be fully themselves, fully rational and loving human beings.[54]

Training

The concentration of MNS members in West Philadelphia also made it possible for the Life Center to serve as a training hub for organizers from around the world. MNS's primary and most enduring contribution to 1970s' social movements was the trainings that it provided to radicals in democratic group process, strategic campaign planning, and direct action tactics. Training collectives devised a series of learning experiences that varied in length from one day to two weeks to an entire year in residence at the Life Center. Other trainers traveled throughout the country, offering "4 x 4" workshops (two intensive four-day

sessions with a break in the middle) to groups of nonviolent organizers working together on a specific campaign
or simply living in the same town.[55] Beyond the specific
content of these trainings, MNS's model of movement
education helped establish a culture of training within the
antiauthoritarian Left that continues to the present day in
the form of DIY skill shares, workshops at anarchist book
fairs, and tactical trainings at convergence centers prior to
large demonstrations.[56]

    The antinuclear power movement came to national
attention in the mid-1970s on the heels of a campaign of
mass nonviolent direct action to resist the development of
the Seabrook nuclear power plant in New Hampshire. As
the movement gained momentum, MNS was instrumen-
tal in both helping participants train for actions and encouraging the movement to structure itself on the basis of
decentralized affinity groups coordinated through directly
democratic spokescouncils.[57] Bookchin, who also played an
important role in the Seabrook campaign, had discovered
the tradition of organizing in affinity groups—small groups
of people with commonalities—in his research into the
Spanish Civil War. At nearly the same time, MNS began
independently promoting small group organizing, based on
observations of how radicals had behaved in mass antiwar
protests in the 1960s and the findings of group psychology
studies that interested some members. Lakey recalls that
MNS first learned of the spokescouncil technique from a
Swedish organizer attending a training at the Life Center
who had used the method in actions to block highway
construction in his own country.[58] MNS trainers traveled

throughout New England in early 1977, facilitating workshops on nonviolent direct action with members and supporters of the largest antinuclear organization on the East Coast, the Clamshell Alliance, which was coordinating the action. On April 30, approximately fourteen hundred people—many of them self-identified anarchists—occupied the site of the proposed power plant, with a thousand or more doing support work. The occupiers were arrested en masse on May 1 and held at five armories nearby.[59]

The mass occupation, which occurred without violence or injury, was a stunning organizational feat in itself. Yet the MNS considered what happened next to be just as powerful and significant. In the armories, MNS members and other action coordinators worked to build jail solidarity—the practice of prisoners bargaining collectively for conditions of their release, rather than being treated individually—and an egalitarian community in microcosm arose during the two weeks that the protesters were held. By facilitating collective decision making on legal strategy using spokescouncils, holding trainings, and encouraging dance parties and other celebrations among the hundreds of detainees, MNS helped turn the incarceration from a repressive act meant to discourage resistance into one of excitement, empowerment, and networking.[60] The Seabrook occupation marked the first time that the three organizational components that have since become de rigueur for antiauthoritarian mass actions—affinity groups, spokescouncils, and consensus process—were used together in the United States. After Seabrook, MNS trainers traveled throughout the country training antinuke organizations in consensus and encouraging them to adopt the spokescouncil model that had worked so well in New Hampshire.

Challenges Arise

By 1976, a number of interrelated problems and tensions had begun to develop within the MNS network. Despite the excitement of the burgeoning antinuke movement, many members felt frustrated with a lack of strategic direction in the organization. While in agreement with MNS's long-term vision, participants were frequently unsure how to best contribute to the variety of movements active at the time. In towns with only a dozen or so MNS members, this lead to a high rate of turnover, as committed organizers moved on to more clearly defined projects; in Philadelphia, some left the Life Center, but many others stayed on, viewing its internal life as the defining aspect of their involvement with radical social change.

At the 1976 Whole Network Meeting, members worked to address the "Philly-centric" way in which MNS was developing by adopting a five-year plan, which encouraged Life Center members to move to promising regions to establish MNS on stronger, less centralized footings. Owing to the plan and interest generated by the important contributions that MNS had made to Seabrook and other high-profile events, the movement grew to a peak of approximately three hundred active members with many more supporters by the decade's end.[61] This thickening of the ranks wouldn't last, however. By the early 1980s, MNS collectives in cities from Chicago to Baltimore had gone through what Twin Cities MNS member Betsy Raasch-Gilman identified as a series of "boom and bust cycles" owing to unresolved questions plaguing the group's work in most parts of the country. "The tension between utopian community and a group of involved activists; the push for perfection in personal and political relationships; the confusion about membership and strategy all could be traced directly to Philadelphia's model," she claimed in retrospect.[62]

In fact, according to Raasch-Gilman, the decline and eventual disbanding of MNS can be attributed to four interrelated factors: a growing emphasis on lifestyle over strategic organizing, the manner in which members carried out antioppression work, weaknesses in the group's decentralized structure, and a fetishization of the consensus decision-making process. Evaluating each of these aspects of MNS's history is complicated because of the decidedly mixed impact each had on the group and the wider antiauthoritarian milieu. MNS pioneered means to respond to problems and limitations that had developed in previous movements, and those methods have had lasting value. At the same time, the group's own history indicates that these innovations included shortcomings of their own, unanticipated by their advocates.

While many found the sense of community that MNS offered the most rewarding part of their involvement, it also lead to serious tensions that eventually contributed to the organization's demise. MNS's prefigurative community attracted some people whose conception of social change diverged sharply from early members' assumptions, while it kept others with shared political commitments away. Its rationale for group living differed in several respects from the often-depoliticized communes and intentional communities formed by counterculturalists in the late 1960s, but this wasn't always obvious. Some visitors believed that an alternative, communal lifestyle constituted a sufficient form of activism. In line with the utopian socialist tradition, they argued that egalitarian communities could serve as a model of the new society, which through their obvious superiority to other ways of life, would naturally attract more participants and inspire imitations.[63]

Lakey remembers encountering newcomers to the Philadelphia Life Center in the mid-1970s who saw it as another intentional community and "wanted lifestyle to be *the* leading edge of change." He had to explain to them that "the cutting edge of [MNS's] understanding of revolution is not lifestyle change. We think of it like ashrams in Gandhi's ideas, which were base camps for revolution. So what do you do in the base camp for revolution? You get ready to go on the barricades."[64] Yet by the late 1970s, the idea that lifestyle change formed the centerpiece of MNS strategy was pervasive both outside and within the organization. A writer for the *Progressive*, for example, described MNS as "Quakers gone counter-cultural."[65] Similarly, when Richard Taylor, a founding member, did not immediately list lifestyle change after being asked to describe aspects of MNS strategy during an interview in the late 1970s, the interviewer prompted him: "One would be lifestyle and modeling." Taylor corrected her, remarking, "Well, one would be working with alternative institutions ..."

creating your own." After further prodding, Taylor conced-
ed, "Lifestyle is important, but it's only one of 5 or 10 key
things . . . it's not more important than non-violent direct
action, or radical caucuses, or alternative institutions."[66]

While the place of lifestyle in MNS strategy was clear
to its founding theorists, not all members and potential
participants were as unambiguous in their thinking, and
the understanding of the role of community building eventually became muddled. By the late 1970s, Raasch-Gilman
saw MNS members fitting into two different categories:
the "hard-bitten shop floor organizers," and the "new age
hippie flakes."[67] Members of the former group spent long
hours encouraging others to participate in pressure campaigns and building coalitions with other organizations,
while the latter prioritized thoroughly changing their own
perceptions and ways of being in the world. The playfully
hyperbolic language in which Raasch-Gilman expressed
this distinction indicates that she (and other members) saw
value in both tendencies, but points to a conceptually useful tension nonetheless.

MNS's commitments to simple living, expanding in-
tramovement jargon, and counterculture-derived social
norms created a subculture that served to glue members together, but also threatened to alienate nonmembers in the
broader Left and the public at large. In September 1976,
Madison, Wisconsin, MNS member Janet Hilliker causti-
cally voiced her concerns regarding the subcultural tendencies growing in MNS in a letter to the network's internal
newsletter. "What responsibility do we have to the many
people who are culturally unlike us?" she asked. "Is our

aim a new uniform society: everyone living in communes, working in food co-ops for lower prices, smoking marijuana, practicing nudity and free love, eating vegetarian, and changing their last names?"[68] It took time for members to see that rather than creating a model of *the* new society, they were establishing one of many possible new lifestyles that grew out of a specific configuration of values that they prioritized. One former member insightfully reflects, "A lot of what was defining our culture was our rebellion against white culture. So, we *were* a counterculture, but we were actually counter to white culture."[69] This made MNS's internal culture less appealing and transformative to people of color, and some white working-class people, who had a different relationship to the dominant, white middle-class culture to begin with.

MNS members certainly were not alone in viewing personal practices and the creation of alternative communities as touchstones of radicalism during the 1970s. Besides the movement centered on establishing rural communes, the ecological and feminist movements that MNS contributed to as well as overlapped with were increasingly focusing on developing alternative culture and community. Prominent members of the Clamshell Alliance, such as Cathy Wolff, "blamed the deterioration of the Clamshell on the turn toward pursuit of community for its own sake," according to Barbara Epstein.[70] Likewise, Alice Echols argues that "cultural feminism"—a form that promoted "new lifestyles within a women's culture, emphasizing personal liberation and growth"—supplanted a more politically confrontational "radical feminism" by 1975.[71] In part, the shift toward new lifestyles was due to exhaustion from the sustained confrontation with political enemies that had marked the second half of the 1960s; it also partly constituted an experiment in innovative approaches to social change for antiauthoritarians within the "new social movements" who sought different goals than traditional leftists had forwarded.

Lifestyle was a strategy advocated in crucial theoretical treatises of the period, including those offered by anarchists. Though in the 1990s he would famously denounce the tendency toward "lifestyle anarchism," Bookchin stated in *Post-Scarcity Anarchism* that "in a more advanced stage of technological development than Marx could have clearly anticipated, a new critique is necessary, which in turn yields new modes of struggle, of organization, of propaganda and of lifestyle." He asserted, "To the degree that workers, vocational students and high school students link their lifestyles to various aspects of the anarchic youth culture, to that degree will the proletariat be transformed from a force for the conservation of the established order into a force for revolution."[72] Bookchin and like-minded thinkers of the time were unable to predict the intensity with which advertising executives of the 1970s would work to recuperate alternative lifestyles, harnessing the desire for self-expression to the needs of capitalism to develop specialized niche markets for its ever-larger array of consumer products, as Thomas Frank and Naomi Klein have since demonstrated.[73]

As the MNS subculture solidified, members noted with growing anxiety that "the center of gravity was no longer in work in popular movements. . . . A quality of introspection became dominant."[74] In part, this inward turn resulted from the increasing focus on what MNS called "oppression/liberation work," or "fighting the -isms." From the outset, MNS members had dedicated energy to developing a deeper collective understanding and approach to combating sexism, gay and lesbian oppression, classism, and racism in the organization as well as their personal lives. These conversations took up more of the group's time and energy as the decade wore on. Committees developed sophisticated analysis of gender, gay and lesbian, and class oppression that sought to understand each within the context of one another, and identified ways in which these social hierarchies were detrimental to all involved, if in different ways and to different degrees. By adding antioppression trainings, based on the group's own experiences, to the workshops it continued to lead, MNS became one of the first organizations to insist that members' "working on their shit"—challenging forms of oppressive personal behavior—was a central task of every radical group, regardless of the immediate concern of its work.

Perhaps inevitably, given the exploratory nature of these efforts, MNS also took wrong turns. At times internal discussions evidenced a tone "shrill in moral judgment," where tendencies soon to be identified with political correctness—such as guilt-inducing righteousness—began to emerge and test the bonds of many local MNS collectives.[75] Simplistic analyses and solutions to social inequalities arose, which indirectly contradicted key aspects of the group's original program. For example, as critiques of classism progressed, the macroanalytic theoretical work that MNS originally prided itself on was increasingly critiqued as middle-class intellectualizing alienating to the working-class members. Strategic campaign planning, meanwhile, was sometimes written off as "a masculine trip" and a "big-bang theory of revolution" where a transfer of power was likened to the male orgasm. (These members argued that as in their idea of a more women-centered sexual practice, more attention should be paid to the process of social change as opposed to simply the end result.)[76] MNS eventually sought to refine ways of accomplishing the goals of soul-searching and changing personal habits, while avoiding the "spiritual dead-end of the blame-and-shame approach." As Lakey put it, this required MNS to make the "decision to become less fascinated with oppression than with liberation."[77]

The growing focus on lifestyle and the emergent critique of strategy in the name of combating privilege amplified challenges arising from MNS's decentralized structure. As a network of semiautonomous collectives, the organization found itself without formal bodies to continue developing theory and political analysis of current events, establish long-term strategy, or help collectives coordinate their activities nationally. Without such structures, long-term campaigns to win reforms and redistribute power to everyday people were on the wane. In January 1977, Dion Lerman wrote, "I feel that MNS needs to be more politically active and more relevant. . . . We are not putting the time and energy that we need to into community and workplace organizing. When we do direct action organizing, which isn't half often enough, we tend to stay in [the] Peace Ghetto, where many MNS people are from, organizing with liberals."[78]

Later that year, in a *Dandelion* article worth quoting at length, Pamela Haines linked MNS's lack of strategic organizing to an unnuanced perspective on leadership developing in the organization:

> Another thing that seems to hold us back is our attitudes about leadership. We have identified the dangers of authoritarian leadership and exposed the sexism that intertwines with it. We have developed more human forms of working together. We have demanded that people change oppressive behavior. But giving up on leadership altogether is a step backwards. The world needs all the good leadership it can get. If each of us avoids taking leadership because we identify it with male chauvinism or authoritarianism or elitism, then we give up part of our human potential—and we give in to our feelings of powerlessness. The result in MNS has been that people have at times held back from taking initiative or stating clearly where they thought the organization should be moving. An unspoken "do-your-own-thingism" has meant that hardheaded decisions about the most effective use of energy have not been made."[79]

Some members tried to combat this tendency by issuing publications such as the pamphlet *Leadership for Change: Toward a Feminist Model*, which insisted on the need for an explicit model of "shared leadership."[80] They noted that despite the disavowal of leaders that had become widespread, various members still carried out what they believed were essential leadership tasks. They did so informally and covertly, though, making the work less accountable and those completing it feel underappreciated.[81] But movement inertia worked against such interventions.

The commitment to consensus decision making also began to hinder the organization. Lakey now states unequivocally: "I think one of the reasons that MNS isn't still around is the downside of consensus."[82] While an organization is new and vital," he argued retrospectively, "consensus decision making can be valuable for encouraging unity. In the longer run, however, consensus can be a conservative influence, stifling the prospects of organizational change."[83] Indeed, the MNS founders originally viewed consensus as a tool that could be useful *in specific situations*. Taylor explained in the late 1970s that consensus had worked for MNS in its early years because those involved in the process shared specific commitments from the outset. Nevertheless, he observed, "I certainly don't feel that consensus ought to be conceived of as sacrosanct, the only way to make decisions, or something like that.... I certainly couldn't see operating all of society on the basis of consensus."[84]

Yet members of MNS elected to use consensus in making all decisions that impacted the network as a whole—including the writing of "official" literature. This process was severely hampered by the principle that any one member could block a group decision, the dispersed and constantly fluctuating nature of the membership, and the state of communication technology. MNS members, of course, did not yet have access to the Internet, but neither did they use conference calling or even speakerphones until the 1980s.[85] Decisions between Whole Network Meetings had to be debated through the internal newsletter and personal mail. This sometimes slowed work to a snail's pace. The refusal to delegate tasks and decisions led, for instance, to MNS taking more than two years to update a brief pamphlet describing the organization's politics.[86] Consensus and full decentralization, innovations designed to make the organization more effective, were beginning to visibly impede the achievement of its goals.

These factors had the combined effect of drawing MNS away from its vision of nonviolent revolution. As Philadelphia member Alan Tuttle wrote in 1977, "The theory and practice of MNS do not coincide. Probably the main area of disparity was in the *talk* of the need for a mass movement and the practice."[87] As early as 1976, Hilliker noted with exasperation that "the aspect of our strategy which encourages active nonviolent revolution is being lost in rhetoric instead of tried out in practice. The multifaceted, balanced strategy we have supported is one for which I've begun to feel an almost desperate need, merging personal with political concerns."[88]

While MNS delved into the lived experience of oppression and focused on ways to not reproduce microhierarchies through its own efforts, the organization devoted less time to a structural analysis of how the same issues were playing out in the larger society. This left MNS insufficiently prepared to strategically respond to developments such as the Reagan administration's assault on the labor movement and welfare state, or the growing right-wing backlash against the gains of the civil rights and feminist movements. As Raasch-Gilman admits, "We did so much difficult internal work because we had such a hard time confronting the larger social, political, and economic world in which we lived. It was easier to try to change ourselves and our immediate comrades than it was to devise long-term campaigns and strategies for changing the outside world."[89]

An Antiauthoritarian Cadre Organization?

In 1982, MNS entered into lengthy discussions about the future of the organization touched off by a statement written by the Baltimore-based Pandora's Collective. The booms and busts that had occurred in many cities shook members' faith that the network was healthy and growing steadily. Meanwhile, the inward gaze of the previous years left many unsure of what MNS's contribution to broader movements was or should be. Two position papers significantly shaped the discussion and decisions that MNS eventually made at its Whole Network Meeting in 1982. The first, drafted by Bill Moyer, encouraged the group to develop from its current "spontaneous" organizational model to an "empowerment" one. The latter would combine the benefits of traditional bureaucratic organizations with those of the spontaneous type that MNS had been up to this point. The new model would seek to develop the abilities and leadership skills of all the group's members, while creating structures allowing the group to establish priorities and carry out long-term work on a national level.[90]

A second paper, Steve Chase's "Reorganizers Manual," provided a useful analysis of tensions within MNS. Chase claimed that when it was formed, MNS intended to be both an "exemplary" and "adversarial" organization. It would be exemplary by living the revolution now through collective living, democratic group process, a rejection of oppressive roles, and support for member's personal growth. It would be adversarial by participating in and training others for strategic campaigns along with direct actions against exploitative corporations, the government war machine, and other unjust institutions. As Chase saw it, by the mid-1970s MNS had begun to lean much more heavily toward the pole of exemplary organization. The intense scrutiny of structure, leadership, and "group dynamics" represented the implicit prioritization of getting the MNS house—the showroom of the new society—in proper order. Chase concluded that this tension left MNS with a fundamental choice about what type of organization it would be: either a loose network of radicals supporting each other's work and commitments to live in a principled fashion, or a "movement-building" cadre organization committed to strategically developing the power of radical social movements in the 1980s.[91]

After considerable discussion, the network meeting accepted core elements of Moyer's and Chase's analyses, agreeing to reshape MNS into a movement-building organization based on an empowerment model. In terms of practical steps, this meant that members committed to carry out three types of work: participation in grassroots organizations, resource sharing with social movements (such as conducting trainings, raising funds, and promoting them in MNS publications), and the building and maintenance of MNS itself. Though an exact definition of an empowerment model of organization was never agreed on, Raasch-Gilman sees it as "one with clear structure, form, goals, and politics which also placed decision-making and control with the lowest possible levels of the group."[92]

During the early 1980s, MNS members devoted considerable energy to new efforts, including Take Back the Night marches, women's peace encampments, and a campaign against the deployment of Cruise and Pershing II missiles coordinated with European organizers. In 1986, however, when members opened a discussion in the pages of the *Grapevine* evaluating the success of becoming a movement-building organization, most were unsatisfied with their progress. The *Organizational Handbook* had been rewritten to reflect the new orientation, and the structure had been finagled, but MNS participation in outside work still occurred individually. Members of MNS put in long hours, for example, in establishing the Pledge of Resistance, an effort to organize thousands of U.S. citizens to commit to nonviolent resistance to direct U.S. military intervention in Central America. But MNS lacked clear ways of contributing to developing struggles *as an organization*. The group, some charged, had not created the means of establishing its own political program or agreeing to specific strategies that members were expected to carry out.[93] With a declining focus on macroanalysis seminars and even informal political conversations, MNS's analysis had not only atrophied but also devolved throughout the 1980s. Chase commented with exasperation, "Ecology . . . was dropped from our official description of the core elements of our philosophy, along with decentralization, cooperative economics, and racial and cultural diversity, when, in 1984, the majority of MNSers agreed to only describe feminism and revolutionary nonviolence as the core elements of our philosophy."[94]

Through another round of searching, participants illuminated a number of underlying causes for the group's inability to meet its goals. Some suggested that many members feared growing, which would threaten the intimate, familial feel that had developed within the tiny organization. Nancy Brigham pointed to an unstated philosophical sticking point: "I think we may have a fundamental contradiction between our agreement to be a movement building organization and a deep belief that having influence is elitist or a misuse of power."[95] Finally, MNS had made little progress in bringing in new members and diversifying itself, due to the defining role that its own movement subculture played in the organization. As Raasch-Gilman perceptively concluded, "We couldn't really expand our cultural boundaries, because our cultural boundaries were what made us who we were."[96]

Despite clarifications and recommitments put forward in 1986, MNS was not able to overcome these internal contradictions. At its network meeting in 1988, the forty assembled members came to consensus to "lay the group down," in the tradition of Quaker committees that have outlasted their usefulness. Doing so, they agreed, would allow them to devote their energy to new efforts able to more effectively meet the political challenges of the 1990s.[97]

MNS and Anarchism, 1988-2008

In 1973, Lakey wrote that MNS was proposing "a revolution which is decisively on the side of life against death, of affirmation rather than destruction. The revolution for life confronts the old order, but confronts lies with openness and repression with community. It shows in its very style how different it is from the necrophilic American Empire."[98] In passages like these, one finds the hippie vocabulary of "affirmation" and "openness" crossed with indictments of the "necrophilic American Empire" that could have been lifted from the lyric sheets of the anarchist punk bands that sprung up in the 1980s. The common thread holding these seemingly different cultural milieus and approaches to change together was the centrality of building community, and the attempt to embody in their "very style" of action how they were different from the present system. Such rhetorical linkages are indicative of the role that MNS played in bridging, transmitting, and transforming the antiauthoritarian politics of the late 1960s into the practices, priorities, assumptions, and attitudes that comprise the contemporary anarchist movement as it has taken shape in the 1980s, 1990s, and 2000s.

When MNS members laid the organization down in 1988, they left in place institutions that later generations of radicals have drawn on. After the organization dissolved, a number of its most committed participants established strategy, direct action, and skills training programs and collectives, such as Training for Change in Philadelphia, Future Now in the Twin Cities, and New Society Trainers in Seattle. New Society Publishers outlived MNS, and continues to publish important titles on feminism, ecology, and social movements, while a summer camp that MNS members founded still provides a safe space for children with queer parents on a sliding-scale fee structure.[99] The area of West Philadelphia that was home to the MNS Life Center became a hub of 1990s' anarchist political activity, and has in recent years become home to a vibrant radical queer community. These developments owe a debt to the infrastructure—collective houses owned by a land trust, a member-operated food co-op, and a community center— left in place by MNS.[100] The low cost of living and sense of political community nourished by these institutions have provided a basis for a number of important interventions, including international organizing to free political prisoner Mumia Abu-Jamal, an innovative ACT-UP chapter that worked to shift attention to the AIDS crisis in the global South, crucial work for media democracy and low-powered FM radio, organizing resistance to the Republican National Convention in 2000, and the promotion of radical Jewish anti-Zionist culture, such as the production in 2004 of the play *An Olive on the Seder Plate*.

Significant as these contributions have been, the ideas that MNS brought to radical politics have made a broader impact than the institutions it left in its wake. Though it is hard to evaluate the exact extent of MNS's influence without fuller accounts of the period's other key organizational initiatives, it is clear that MNS was a major innovator and force in promoting, among other tools and approaches: multi-issue political analysis, consensus process, collective living and political community in urban areas, modeling political commitments in everyday relationships and life choices, network structure, internal antioppression work, identity-based caucuses, cost sharing and sliding-scale prices, direct action, and the use of spokescouncils.

The influence of MNS's approach to activism in recent times was perhaps most evident in the manner in which organizing for the actions against the World Trade Organization took place in Seattle in 1999. This is unsurprising, as former MNS members, including Raasch-Gilman, along with organizers heavily influenced by MNS, such as Starhawk and David Solnit, played central roles in developing the actions and trainings for participants. In Seattle, the nonviolent direct action tradition that MNS promoted intertwined and sometimes conflicted with other tactics and tendencies of the antiauthoritarian Left—for example, ecodefense monkey wrenching and Autonomen-style black blocs—that had developed parallel to the MNS project, giving a sense of how complex and variegated the movement has become since 1968.

But if the success of Seattle demonstrates the clear debts and respect owed to MNS members and their milieu by contemporary antiauthoritarians, the challenges that quickly emerged in the North America global justice movement following Seattle make it equally clear that radicals have not learned to avoid the pitfalls of the MNS experience, much less develop workable solutions to the problems that eventually sunk the MNS ship. How could an antiauthoritarian movement create theory and strategy on a national (or even international) basis? What role did and

should explicit and implicit leadership play in the movement? How to deal with the relative racial and class homo-
geneity of the participants? And how to work productively
with other radical and progressive sectors? These issues
were all under debate before the 9/11 attacks sideswiped
the movement and changed the conversation. The fact that
these questions will reoccur, and continue to weigh down
the efforts of new movements and generations of radicals
until they are more adequately addressed, has been made
apparent by the experience of the reformed SDS. In an as-
sessment of that organization's first two years, Joshua Kahn
Russell and Brian Kelly list an array of frustrating inclina-
tions and practices that SDS has had to confront:

> When there were too many male voices represent-
> ing SDS in the media, the response was to attack
> those speaking rather than to create systems of sup-
> port for others to publish and be represented. . . .
>
> People proposed [organizational] structures
> that were rarely designed to meet concrete needs.
> The debate was often framed by concepts like "de-
> centralization" versus "centralization"—an abstract
> theoretical simplification. . . .
>
> Informal networks based on experience and
> personal relationships emerged . . . whispers and
> groaning about informal leadership permeated the
> convention floor.[101]

It is striking and disappointing, but perhaps not surprising, to note the extent to which these conversations

follow those occurring within MNS in 1976.

Some recent anarchist theory likewise optimistically promotes a version of MNS strategy with little consideration of the substantial problems that MNS encountered when it tried to enact such a strategy. For example, in *Gramsci Is Dead: Anarchist Currents in the Newest Social Movements*, Richard Day presents a wide-ranging and insightful history of anarchist and related political thought from the early nineteenth century to the contemporary period.[102] Yet Day concludes this itinerary by explicitly rejecting strategic organizing campaigns that seek to directly confront inequalities of power and wealth, in favor of focusing overwhelmingly on building prefigurative institutions. For Day, "nothing is more important today than building, linking and defending autonomous communities," so that in the gaps and margins of the neoliberal order, "spaces are available for experimentation" with forms like autonomous zones and intentional communities.[103]

In 1933, the young anarchists who comprised the Vanguard Group criticized the tendency of movement veterans to live in anarchist "colonies," or intentional communities, and claim such activity as revolutionary. A defender of such colonies asked in a letter to the group's journal, "Isn't a living experiment superior to any logical proof, and doesn't the value of colony building lie exactly in the fact that it tries to solve social questions by experiments and not by arguments only?" The Vanguard Group pointedly responded:

> There is too much superstitious awe about the word experiment. An experiment . . . cannot be

indefinitely pursued without taking stock of all the previous failures and without introducing a certain variant in each and every attempt. The history of such attempts, for nearly a century, to solve the so-cial problem via colony building has clearly shown the futility of such a method. To keep repeating the same attempts without an intelligent appraisal of all the numerous failures in the past is not to uphold the right to experiment, but to insist upon one's right to escape from the hard facts of social struggle into the world of wishful belief.[104]

MNS knew in theory, from the outset, that alternative community building was an insufficient means of creating revolutionary change, even if, to the regret of many partici-pants, the group ended up emphasizing community and lifestyle in practice. The members' subsequent experience confirmed the insufficiencies of an overreliance on prefigu-rative projects. For Day and others to ignore the lessons that MNS and similar efforts offer is to neglect the true meaning of "experiment" noted by the Vanguard Group.

A key tenet that MNS lived by in its earlier years stated, "Most of what we need to know about making a nonviolent revolution, we have yet to learn." The disap-pointing setbacks that our movements—whether com-mitted to nonviolence or not—have faced in recent years seem to indicate the continuing validity of such a proposi-tion. Still, it seems clear that a good deal of what we have to learn can be gained from studying the specific successes and shortcomings of sympathetic movements not just in the nineteenth and early twentieth centuries but also in the recent past—and then modifying our practice accordingly. MNS was an essentially anarchist organization that for seventeen years claimed hundreds of members in more than a dozen cities and contributed to most of the significant struggles of its day. Furthermore, it was perhaps the only such organization, in its time and since, to forward a comprehensive vision and strategy for making antiauthoritarian revolutionary change in the late twentieth-century United States. As such, it deserves to be not only remembered out of respect but also studied assiduously by contemporary antiauthoritarians, so that we might take stock and introduce new variants into each and every one of *our* new efforts. As MNS illustrates, when we don't learn from our mistakes, we haven't fully learned from our great successes.

CONVERSATIONS

Nonviolence, Consensus, and Leadership: An Interview

I n June 2007, Andrew Willis Garcés and I interviewed George Lakey as part of our exploration of MNS's history. The following excerpts from that interview speak to questions of tactics, decision making, and organization that radicals struggle with today. Before cofounding MNS, Lakey worked as a trainer at the Martin Luther King School of Social Justice. In 1992 he launched Training for Change, a movement education center that carries on MNS's commitment to educate organizers from around the world in campaign strategy, popular education techniques, and more. A professor at Swarthmore College, his most recent book is *Facilitating Group Learning: Strategies for Success with Adult Learners* (Jossey-Bass, 2010).

MNS advocated nonviolent revolution. What makes someone a nonviolent revolutionary versus a pacifist?

LAKEY: Pacifism is hugely influenced by conflict aversion. It really shows its middle classness in that way. There is a tremendous level of yearning for harmony because many pacifists see conflict itself as the problem. On the other hand, nonviolent revolutionaries welcome conflict, depend on it, and see polarization as absolutely essential. Whereas most pacifists hate polarization, we welcome it as long as polarization happens in such a way that we're on the winning side! And then, of course, lots of pacifists are OK with capitalism, and nonviolent revolutionaries are not. They are strongly anticapitalist, and often antistate.

Why would someone who believes in nonviolence naturally oppose capitalism and the state? What's the linkage?

I think Gandhi said it best: "Inequality is a form of violence, and requires violence to defend itself." On the political front, that implicates certain types of states, and that certainly is the nature of capitalism—to create inequalities.

MNS placed a lot of emphasis on "process"—on the way in which the group made decisions and carried out its work. One of the abiding influences of MNS on contemporary antiauthoritarian movements is the importance placed on consensus decision-making processes. How did process become central to everything MNS did?

There were a number of influences. Some of us had been involved in Mississippi Freedom Summer [a crucial campaign of the black freedom movement in which northern college the Madison people who invited us there were affiliated with the Center for Conflict Resolution, whose specialty was consensus. They were saying, "Consensus is the way to go, the feminist way to go." Another formative influence in the 1970s was the Federation of Egalitarian Communities. They were heavy into consensus, and many people flowed through them and were influenced by them. So that was another standard setter maybe. There was a sense that if you were really radical, really willing to leave the capitalist cutthroat world, then consensus was part of the package—that's what community really means.

Many contemporary activists now believe that consensus and affinity groups are crucial forms of organization, but they don't believe in nonviolence. Did you see those things—consensus and nonviolence—as integrally linked?

Consensus is a structural attempt to get equality to happen in decision making, so it's very much about equality. So again, back to Gandhi: where we are pushing equality, we are pushing nonviolence. Where we are allowing or encouraging inequality, there is a violent backup there somewhere, even though it might be masked. Affinity groups speak to the question of hierarchy. The more affinity groups proliferate (plus other things being true), the less we need hierarchical, top-down control of social movements, the more nonviolent those movements are likely to be. That is, I think hierarchy promotes violence internally in order to maintain itself. Like, sooner or later [Hugo] Chavez will probably live out the nightmare that the Beltway is trying students helped African American Mississippians organize for voting rights in 1964]. So we thought, "Of course, participatory democracy!" Yet even though we yearned for community and experienced it in fleeting moments during the 1960s, a lot of our nature was individualistic. So we named it. We said, "Look, we have not been brought up to be communitarians, truly collective beings." We realized that the price of survival with all the egomaniacs [in the group] was going to be an explicit process. Also, some of us were influenced by A. J. Muste, who had had a really bruising experience with [authoritarian decision-making structures] even before the 1960s, especially during his time in the Trotskyist movement. So we also had some lore from elders to help us realize we were going to need a big process renovation to be able to cohere at all.

Now, how do we make decisions? From the get-go, as we created a community of people interested in exploring the idea of living together and practicing the revolution, I don't even remember it being explicitly discussed. I remember it being a shared understanding, and that was probably the Quaker influence. There were a whole bunch of Quakers involved, and it was just assumed that whatever we'd end up with we would have arrived at by consensus. (The thing that is tricky about that is that we were in formation, which means anybody who could see the direction that we were going and didn't like it could just not come to the next meeting. So that's like attrition rather than consensus!) But then, I think we formally decided that consensus would be our process of decision making in our first National Network Meeting, which was in Madison. And to create for him. Despite all the populism, hierarchy has this influence, and hierarchs end up using violence as a way to try to keep themselves in power.

Today, a lot of radicals of our generation see consensus as the only legitimate way to make decisions, no matter what task or kind of activity they are working on. Likewise, decentralized affinity groups and spokescouncils are often viewed as the only valid way of organizing for revolutionary change. What do you think the lesson of MNS should be about the uses and shortcomings of those forms?

I think that one of the reasons that MNS isn't still around is the downside of consensus. I was never a fanatical consensus person because I thought there was a big difference between my Quaker practice and political practice. I thought there were times where consensus would be just right and other times when it wouldn't be. But I was charmed by Seabrook in the sense of, "Hey, let's see how far we can take this." MNS was a lab. We thought, "Let's try it here and try it there, and see how it serves and how it doesn't."

But eventually people started getting rigid about it. The metaphor I used to use was: we fitted out a pretty good ship, and launched it in the direction of someplace. But the rudder was fixed. So long as we were going in a direction we wanted to go in, and there weren't a lot of icebergs cropping up, we could just keep doing that. However, what about when we needed to make really big changes, like the Titanic would have benefited from? We weren't able to do it because the ability to block consensus was available to, really, anybody. I got really frightened about this when I heard some of our newer members explaining that the main benefit of being a member of MNS was, "You get to block consensus!" By the late 1980s, a huge shift had happened in the movement to make it *the* way to make decisions. So I think in the 1970s it was cutting edge, and in the 1980s it was settling in to *the* way, and people had to argue for parliamentary procedure if they wanted to do it.

How do you think that shift happened, so that in some sectors of the Left consensus became hegemonic, and came to be what made you a radical or not a radical?

My first thought would be a combination of the women's movement and antinuke movement. The antinuke movement proved its viability among people who weren't ideologically on the same page. And the women's movement brought righteousness, as with everything they did. It was the correct way to make decisions . . . to liberate the voices of all.

Let's talk about the idea of living the revolution now or what today is often called prefigurative politics. How did MNS decide that was important, and what were some of the benefits?

I think there were several impulses that lead to it. One that weighed heavily with me was a sense of demoralization that came out of the 1960s. Many felt it was all over and we'd failed. So how do you start something new in a largely demoralized bunch of activists? We needed confidence-building measures. We needed to know that we could do something *now* as well as project a vision and strategy. Another impulse was making a living. We didn't picture being a fund-raising organization with that subsidizing the activists. Activists had to provide their own income. But by living communally, the costs go way down. So some people said, "We love the idea of printing, so how about we start a collective print shop?" And that was employment for a lot of people. And a couple other people said, "The cheaper we can get quality food, the better, so let's start a co-op." Cheap food, that's great, and livelihood for the people who'd be managers. We had a chance to create something and make it work, and provide some benefit to the neighborhood. So I think several agendas came together around prefigurative politics.

One aspect of MNS was building alternative institutions. But there was also the idea of living your life differently, according to different values—including living and not just working collectively. This seems to be another legacy of MNS. Was there an assumption that by living in new ways, other people would see the value and change their own lives in accordance?

This is a great question because this was the parting of the ways between those of us who stuck and many people who had MNS on their list of egalitarian communities to go around to. I don't know how many people I talked to who said, "I've just been to Acorn, I've just been to Twin Oaks, and here I am. What do you got?" And I'd say, "Probably not something you'd like. Because the cutting edge of our understanding of revolution is not lifestyle change. We think of it like ashrams in Gandhi's ideas—the ashrams that he set up, which were base camps for revolution. So what do you do in the base camp for revolution? You get ready to go on the barricades. You're getting ready to go to jail on the ashrams. And that's what we are doing." And so a lot of people would say, "Thank you for not wasting my time. I'm out of here." They wanted lifestyle to be the leading edge of change, and we clearly were not doing that.

For us the cadre model was really important. Our role in the neighborhood safety group, our role in the food co-op, our role in the antinuke movement was not to get people to buy our lifestyle. That's not the point. Now if they happen to see that we're doing effective work side by side with them and they say, "It's funny, we're in this discouraging period and I'm feeling it's all over, and you're not feeling despair," maybe that's an opening. You can talk about why you don't come to the meetings in despair. So it's not that we are closed or closeted about it, but you have to figure out how to be accessible enough to connect with other people.

Another former member, Betsy Raasch-Gilman, claims that MNS had "a positive allergy to leadership." For many young radicals today leadership is still anathema. When MNS was founded, what was the understanding of the role of leadership and leaders within the group? How did that change over seventeen years?

My recollection of the early days of MNS was not allergy to leadership but a growing weariness of *male* leadership. So I think the questioning of leadership in the early MNS was much more coming from a feminist place. And often when criticism of leadership behavior happened, it would be of masculine styles. Some members wrote a wonderful article called "Speaking in Capital Letters." It argued that the way men in mixed groups tend to prevail, or try to prevail, is that they say everything emphatically as if it's been thought about for months, even though they're making it up in the moment! So there was a lot of criticism of leadership *behaviors*, but it was put in a feminist context, which implied that we need strong women leaders who will have different styles sometimes, and this led to some amazing things happening. A group of women got together and requested-slash-demanded that I give them a seminar on political theory, because that was an arena they felt like they needed to catch up on with male leaders of MNS. And we didn't talk about the fact that I, a male, was giving a seminar to women on political theory. In a lot of circles that would sound terrible. But we just saw it as skill transfer or knowledge transfer. Five years later I wouldn't have been able to do it because, in addition to being weary about George, Bill, Dick, and so on, on the grounds that we are all men, the criticism had shifted to the fact that we were providing leadership at all. Who needs leaders?

So that changed in five years? What were the roots of that change?

That's really complicated. There were a few things. I think it was the communitarians, in part. Because there were communitarians that went off to Twin Oaks or wherever, but there were actually others who thought, "Yep, this [MNS] is a great setup. And we don't mind going to demonstrations now and then." So people were coming to MNS who weren't that involved in strategic political work. [Their idea of] living the revolution now was their big draw.

Another issue was each wave of "ism" that we responded to. Feminism was the first one, then homophobia was the one we tackled, then classism and racism. Each one of those raised more personal growth issues for each of us. There are the men and women saying, "Oh my god, I had no idea how sexist I was. Oh, but look how homophobic I am!" The personal growth dimension constantly got refreshed and had a sense of urgency for us, living in community, by our increasing awareness. So we had tons of work to do. And that was important work, but it was different from organizing campaigns that require a different kind of leadership.

And another thing that was going on was this consensus principle, which at first was very much about a seeking. Another of our catchphrases was, "The wisdom of the whole is wiser than the wisdom of the wisest member." We were going after the wisdom. It's really different when a group is seeking wisdom through consensus, and when a group is making a decision, and it's like, "You've said enough. This is the third time you've spoken!" "Yeah, but he happens to have done co-ops for twenty years, and we're talking about the co-op now!" "It's the third time he's spoken!"

It sounds like the formality of it, rather than the underlying motivation behind the process, took over.

The culture just really shifted. At one point, an organizational development consultant volunteered to work with MNS because it seemed as an organization we were getting sick. She had us do an exercise where she said, "All of you who are leaders in the organization, you go over there." So like three people, blushing, go across the room. And she smiled and said, "OK, all of you who do covert leadership, you go over here." And about a third of the room gets up, including me, and goes over there. So it turned out there was this group of covert older male leadership—and this is so traditionally male, too, like we're holding the family together. So that's what we were doing, but not even talking to each other about it. It was just so fucked up. I got us to be a men's group for two years, and we cried a lot with each other about how we didn't want to be covert and have to manipulate to keep an organization afloat because we can't come out of our closets as resourceful people. I kept saying, "What if we were to look at leadership as resources. And it depends on the issue. Like, on this issue you know more and I know less, and on another issue it's different." So we're scanning constantly for the most resources we could bring to bear on this decision.

As someone at the heart of one of the groups that is perceived as one of the most antileader organizations in recent history, what would you say to young organizers today who see having defined leaders as undesirable or reactionary?

Our experience says it doesn't pay to be antileadership. It does pay to believe in shared leadership and look at

leadership as a concept of resources rather than as the likeli-
hood of domination.

A couple of cofounders of MNS had been on Dr.
King's national staff in the civil rights movement. They saw,
up close and personal, what it is like to rely on a charismatic figure. Even though they and other founders of MNS
were in love with Dr. King, we also saw the tremendous
vulnerability that produces in a movement and realized we
needed to create a leadership understanding that did not
rely on charismatic leaders. But actually I think we went
too far. We went reactive to the point where some thought,
"Well, if you have charisma, don't bother to come by here!"
I'm really glad that we understood that the whole question
of leadership needs to be taken up. We went quite far on
leadership issues in our laboratory experiments and we also
didn't go far enough, and that's what did us in.

Looking back, one difference between the period of the
1970s and today is we were still close to genuinely inspirational leadership in the 1970s—that is to say, Dr. King,
Nelson Mandela, and some of the people around them.
And that stirred our blood, however critical we were of the
structural weaknesses that went with that. A lot of us activists yearn to be able to give our all in an exemplary way, to
somehow live out our highest aspirations, and live them out
in the political realm. And I think that when a figure like
that comes along, it elevates the discourse and aspiration of
people. It's easier for us to try to hold ourselves in a higher
place. I wouldn't have predicted I would say this in response
to this question, but this is what's coming out. It may be
temperamental; it may have to do with that sector of the

population, like me, who respond to human beings being exemplary. Maybe other people are more inspired by books or collectives moving in history or right now. But there is some batch of folks, like me, who toot some on the saxophone, but when we hear in a jazz club a group really getting down, we walk out of there somehow expanded. I think that those of us who were close to the 1970s saw a lot of the expanded behavior, expanded performance, in the realm of political action. That was part of the texture of our consciousness.

And I don't see that today. The quality of political leadership in the United States has just been so abysmal. I think on the radical side as well as on the liberal side. Abysmal is too strong a word. But what I'm trying to point out is a lack of figures who rise above, who are like that jazz club performance group that get into the zone, who make us say, "Yes, maybe I can get into the zone someday." I don't run into that condition culturally, and I don't run into activists very often who can tell me the last time that they've been to that jazz club and have been lifted in that way.

You've been involved in antiauthoritarian social movements for five decades. Is there anything unique to you about the younger organizers you've worked with recently or the political movements in which they are taking action?

There are some really positive, inspirational developments. For one thing, all this awareness of oppression/liberation issues. In the 1970s, just taking on feminism was a huge, huge thing. And now we've got so many young people who understand a bunch of "isms" and relationships among the "isms" at some level in their cognitive map, if not all the way through. Also in the 1970s, there were still a lot of young activists who believed that the United States wasn't structurally corrupted to its core by imperialism. They could still hold on to a belief that Vietnam was in some way an aberration, or maybe it was an extreme of tendencies that could be found in other ways in Latin America or whatever. But it seems to me that younger activists are far more ready today to make a sweeping analysis. And then of course the environmental picture. When we were starting in the 1970s, few people shared our view. And now, even Al Gore does! [*Laughs*] So there are some real pluses in the way people start out today.

Reflections by Former MNS Members

On March 10 and 11, 2010, former MNS members Nancy Brigham, Bob Irwin, George Lakey, Betsy Raasch-Gilman, and Lynne Shivers spoke about their experiences and answered questions at public meetings held in New York City and Philadelphia. Below I have combined and edited the transcripts of those events. In a few instances, I asked the presenters to elaborate on important ideas that they could not fully develop at the meetings due to time constraints. Biographical notes precede the remarks of each participant, save for Lakey, who was introduced above.

George Lakey

There's so much to say about the birth and death of MNS, and I'm not going to be able to say it all. The birth of anything new is influenced by what has preceded it. The founders of MNS were enormously influenced by our experiences in the 1960s—both by things that worked well and those that didn't. We realized that there were a lot of people burning out toward the end of the 1960s, and we thought individualism had something to do with that. There were other causes as well. We noticed that there were ways in which movements of the 1960s ran up against brick walls, and couldn't analyze those walls. The places where activists had been used to turning for radical analysis, like Leninism, weren't really providing the guidance that we felt we needed. So we were stimulated to do something new, but to do it in a way that spoke to our personal conditions and also to the idea deficit that we felt existed in the beginning of the 1970s.

I'd been working in Europe for a year. When I returned and did a quick scan of what was going on in this country, I realized that the organization I'd been working with, A Quaker Action Group, was itself running out of gas. I thought, "What a good chance to start something new. Maybe I can find some forces that would like to work together, but might need to be pushed together in order to work together." Because so often there's strong egos involved in everything that's out there, politically. I found that there was a radical caucus within the largest peace organization in the country, the American Friends Service Committee, trying to push it to the left. There were also some young Quakers, who were utopians, who were forming communities. They were really tuned into deep ecology at the time. The hard core of A Quaker Action Group was still persevering and was ready for something new. Finally, around the country, so many independent young people were feeling disappointed that they missed the 1960s—that they missed the party. They had gotten there too late and were wondering, "How can we learn and act and be part of the great heroic legacy of trying to turn this country into one that we can be really proud of?" Trying to put those four elements together was not easy, but we were able to start.

One of the things that we really needed was a departure from the old hierarchical, top-down, organization politics that more or less dominated the 1960s. Fortunately, while I was in Europe I found an anarchist organization in the Netherlands called Shalom. They had created a successful horizontal network of autonomous groups that were both doing prefigurative work and also doing action work. I thought, "Maybe this is an organizational model that will enable the somewhat-disparate groups to be able to work together." So that's where we got that model, starting out from another country.

While organizing, we visited the War Resisters League and some of the circles of radical pacifists, both anarchist and socialist, because we didn't want them to feel as though we were in competition—that we were trying to tread on their turf. We made up an agreement not to bad-mouth each other. I know you've never heard of radicals bad-mouthing each other, but we thought somebody might start that as a new practice, and we didn't want to encourage that! [*Laughter*] In retrospect, we could have reached out much further, but at least we weren't trying to start this thing as another great idea hatched in somebody's attic or cellar, while totally forgetting about the rest of the movement.

We grew rapidly in the beginning. So we began to think, "Maybe this *is* going to be a movement for a new society, and maybe these organizational structures that we're coming up with could be the new wine skin—they could contain the wine of our new ideas. Maybe these structures could pervade mass movements that form in the 1970s!" The environmental movement was growing, and the women's movement was growing rapidly. We thought maybe our offerings to them would be eagerly grabbed, and we would really become a movement for a new society as a mass phenomenon. But that did not happen.

So we settled into an alternative version of what we were trying to do, which was to create a cadre organization of people who would think of themselves as basically full-time revolutionaries. David McReynolds, my old friend from the War Resisters League, used to call us Bolsheviks because, in truth, we wanted to be professional revolutionaries. We wanted to somehow piece together a way of living that would enable us to basically be full-time revolutionists. Then our way of trying to make social change would not only be through organizational experiments that would demonstrate the effectiveness of non-hierarchical forms and the feminist spirit living within groups themselves. We would also engage in struggles through peoples' movements that were springing up in response to crises, and we would permeate those movements. But the difference between us and the Bolsheviks was that the Bolsheviks were willing to manipulate their way into influencing mass movements, and we said no to manipulation. We took seriously Gandhi's admonition that what you do now, actually becomes causative in the future—that there isn't really a distinction between ends and means in that way. We believed that we needed to relate to movements in a respectful way. What we would bring would be skills, some ideas, and some training. We'd bring the effective use of nonviolent direct action from the 1960s and the various campaigns we'd worked on, but we would do it in a respectful way.

One of the things that really motivated us, both in terms of our relations to the outside world and also internally, is that we believed that most of what we need to know in order to bring about a nonviolent revolution we have yet to learn. We really felt humbled. It wasn't just a pose. We felt like there was so much changing—multinational corporations taking on the world in much bolder ways, the environmental changes occurring, the deepening understanding of the "isms" that oppress us. All of this meant new theory and new practice would need to be evolved, and therefore, we couldn't afford to be arrogant. We needed to actually be on as rapid a learning curve as we could be, and we were constantly challenging ourselves to learn as rapidly as possible. And as we were bringing whatever experiments, skills, and knowledge to broader movements, we realized that our main way of influencing the world was through our creativity. At a particular moment when a movement was up against a particular obstacle, it was our creativity at being able to adapt ideas or come up with new ideas that was going to be helpful to people.

Now I get to the death part. In the mid-1980s or so, a number of us started to feel that we were losing our creativity. To recapture creativity, we would have to go through a renewal of the organization itself. So we made a big effort at both organizational changes and also changes with regard to our demographic base. As you can tell from what I said in the beginning, we were a counterculture. We were pushing, pushing, pushing mainstream liberals, and positioning ourselves as counter to the folks who were accepting way too many assumptions about American empire, the environment, and so on. The trouble with being a counterculture is that you taste and smell and act, in some ways, like the culture that you're counter to.

We started out as a white group that actually had a lot of its leadership from working-class people, but had a middle-class tone. We were a white counterculture to a white culture. And so as part of our renewal effort, we realized, "Whoa, how can we possibly be the movement we want to be if we're not multiracial?" So we went on a campaign to extend our cultural boundaries. We realized that with our failure to do that, we were just tasting and smelling too much like a white counterculture. But this was difficult. For one thing, our friends who were in the black counterculture were black nationalists, and they were in part rebelling against the black mainstream. So sociologically we felt trapped, and that was one of the reasons we decided to give up the farm.

In 1988, we decided to lay ourselves down because we realized that the multiracial organizations of the future needed to be built from the ground up in a multicultural context. Unlike a lot of the organizations that I've known that might have benefited from laying themselves down, we actually went ahead and did it. But we did it with a lot of dignity and a lot of pride, a lot of self-respect. We did a lot of grieving because we were a community. We were sisters and brothers; we were close comrades. And so we did it with a lot of respect for each other, but we said, "Let's let it go."

Betsy Raasch-Gilman

Raasch-Gilman spent eleven years in MNS. She has worked as a food co-op coordinator; served briefly as a hospital chaplain; was a member of the Northland Poster Collective; and currently makes her living as a self-employed bookkeeper. Training in nonviolent direct action is still her major passion, which she does under the umbrella of Training for Change.

I'm going to talk about what MNS did and what I see as our impact on wider movements. The first thing I want to talk about is the *Strategy for a Living Revolution*, a book that George wrote early in the life of MNS. He laid out a strategy for creating a nonviolent revolution in the United States, and there were five basic parts of that strategy. The first three tasks were: building strong people's organizations, cultural preparation for revolution, and action for revolutionary reform, which he originally called "propaganda of the deed." We thought those three tasks needed to be repeated over and over again in order for there to be the mass base for a massive nonviolent revolution in the United States. At the point when there's enough opposition built up, we can withdraw our cooperation from the structure. It's really our cooperation that keeps the structure in place. So mass strikes, mass boycotts, non-cooperation with military authorities—all kinds of things are possible at that point, and that's what brings a government down. That has happened, and in the book George pointed out a number of examples. It's happened even more since he wrote that book.

The final stage is really important too. That's what he called "parallel institutions." If we're going to create a power vacuum, if we're going to take down a structure or system, we have to have something ready to go into its place. Because if there is a power vacuum, a counterrevolution will start immediately. That's a given. We have to have something that puts the system in place that we really want to live in. Whether that's a government or a nongovernment system, we still have to have the pieces ready to put into effect and in place.

So those are the five stages, or paths, in creating a revolution, as we saw it. Obviously the task of overthrowing the government of the United States is unfinished, OK? [*Laughter*] MNS did not finish it, but that's what we were working on. That's how we saw ourselves able to bring about a nonviolent revolution here.

Although George published that book early on, it did take us a while to work into that strategy. Some of the initial projects that were worked on in MNS on the East Coast were ones that they initiated. There was a blockade of the port of Philadelphia to prevent the shipment of weapons to Pakistan that spread to the port of Baltimore, and other ports up and down the East Coast. That was something that MNS initiated. There was a street safety program in West Philadelphia that MNS initiated. Another example is the Philadelphia-Namibia Action Group in solidarity with the people of Namibia, which was then a territory occupied by apartheid South Africa. These were things that we started— really important projects for people around the world and in Philadelphia—but they weren't exactly what *Strategy for a Living Revolution* laid out, because we weren't participating in an existing people's movement. However, we did eventually work our way into that strategy.

The big change was in 1977. In the small town of Seabrook, they were building a nuclear power plant. The company had cleared the land for the construction of the nuclear power plant, and antinuclear activists were trying to prevent this thing from being built. They had gone through the court system and lost all the court battles. In 1977, fourteen hundred activists brought their tents and their sleeping bags to the location where that power plant was going to be built and occupied it. And of course they were arrested. They were carted off to five different National Guard armories. MNS contributed to this action in several ways. First of all, we did some of the nonviolence training for this action in the beginning. But the more important contribution happened inside the armories. Some activists were held for two weeks before they were arraigned and released, but those two weeks were like a long training session. They created self-organized study groups, and self-organized seminars and workshops. They used spokescouncils for everybody who was in each armory. Affinity groups would appoint one person to be part of a spokescouncil, and that was a rotating position. Those armories were essentially autonomous zones because the so-called prisoners were calling the shots. They decided whether or not, how much, and how far to obey the orders given by the guards. MNS contributed to all of that—the preparation and then what happened when people were in the armories.

People had come from all over the country to occupy Seabrook. When they were released, they largely plead guilty so that they wouldn't have to deal with the court battles afterward. And then they went home and started organizing their own antinuclear alliances. They came to the Twin Cities and organized the Northern Sun Alliance, went to Wisconsin and organized the Northern Thunder Alliance, and went to California and organized the Abalone Alliance. So MNS's skills, process, and nonviolence trainings expanded astronomically, because they were taken to all parts of the country by the people who had been in the armories in Seabrook. It was a tremendous success for us in terms of jump-starting an antinuclear movement. It also coincided with an initiative within MNS to decentralize our efforts. We wanted to start pushing out into the rest of the country, starting little MNS communities and Life Centers. That's where I came in because I was living in Saint Paul and I was recruited for MNS there.

Seabrook was a big change in the way that we participated in people's movements. From there on, we worked in a whole number of movements during the 1980s. I'm just going to mention a few of them. There was a big antinuclear weapons movement, and MNS participated in it quite actively. Part of that involved women's peace encampments—women going to army bases and weapons factories, and setting up camps outside them to demonstrate, "We want peace, we don't want nuclear weapons, we don't want to train people to use nuclear weapons, we don't want nuclear war." Later on, there was a real danger that the Reagan administration was going to invade Nicaragua in Central America because of the Marxist revolution there in 1979. A Central American solidarity movement evolved in the United States to prevent that kind of an invasion, and MNS contributed to that. George Willoughby was one of the initiators of Peace Brigades International, which created another innovation with nonviolence, asking people in the global North to go to the global South and escort activists who are in danger because of their activism. Those are some of the ways we impacted the movements while we were alive as an organization.

I also just want to say a word about personal growth within MNS. An important aspect is how we worked on the oppression issues that we had identified. Feminism impacted MNS from the beginning as it raised issues about who gets credit for what, what is leadership, and what is political work. Feminism challenged everybody to take a look at their sexist behaviors, and their internalized sexism and homophobia.

We also did a lot of work about classism. We asked why middle-class values and upper-middle-class values are so important even in the movement. How do working-class and poor people claim their rightful place in a movement organization? We developed a couple of practical responses to classism. One was cost sharing. We decided to cost share when we got together in network meetings or training programs. We cost shared not just the costs of the training but also the cost of what it took us to get there and occasionally even our lost wages. So if you wanted to come to an MNS gathering, we said don't stay away because you can't afford it. If you came to a gathering and you really couldn't afford it, you might actually go home with money in your pocket. People who traveled a short distance to get there might end up paying for three or four people to get there because they had the resources to do it. This was one of the most challenging processes we used, but it also really raised the level of true solidarity among us. In some of our communities, we also had a mutual aid fund. People who had a little bit of extra money put it into an account in the bank, and anybody within the MNS community who needed money could withdraw it. It was no questions asked: if you needed the money, it was there. We shared that way.

Looking back over our internal newsletters, we probably spent as much time working on racism as practically any of the other oppression issues. But we largely spun our wheels about it. Starting in about 1984, it became more and more apparent to us that a multicultural (that's the term we used then) organization was what was going to be most important to bringing about the kinds of changes that we wanted to see in the United States. We decided we couldn't really call ourselves revolutionary if we were totally white. So given that we were unable culturally to make the changes that would be necessary to become a not-majority-white organization, we decided to give up and see what else we could do. That's the quick overview of how we impacted the world.

Nancy Brigham

Brigham joined Philadelphia MNS and the Life Center in Fall 1972. She helped develop and promote the macroanalysis seminars and two-week general training programs. Brigham was later involved in a succession of MNS network communication and coordination efforts.

I'm going to talk about MNS's evolving organizational structures. We wanted to be a decentralized organization. We wanted the power to be at the grass roots, but with coordination where we needed coordination. From the beginning we saw ourselves as an experiment in organization because there were not a lot of models for this kind of thing out there. There were a lot of hierarchical organizations, but that was not what we wanted to do.

In terms of people joining MNS, membership was through being part of a collective; it wasn't individual. We used a process called clearness, which meant that if you wanted to join a particular group, you would meet with that group, or maybe a subset of that group, to say, "Here's what I'm thinking. Here's why I'm interested in joining. Here's what I have to bring. Here are my questions." And collectives would join the MNS network through the same process. We would have a discussion, back and forth, to decide if it was a good match and if it made sense.

MNS had three different kinds of working collectives. One was direct participation in grassroots organizations and social movements. Second was resource sharing with local movements, which included training, creating all the literature, macroanalysis seminars, and those kinds of things. The third kind of collective work was the actual organizational maintenance and development of MNS. I think that's the one in which we struggled the most from the beginning, so I'm going to talk a little bit more about our experiments in that third area.

We had these collectives in Philadelphia and other places, and we first tried to organize ourselves into regional networks. The idea of bioregionalism wasn't quite in the forefront as much as it has been since, but we were definitely thinking regionally. In many places we did periodically have regional gatherings, but except in Philadelphia, we had a hard time sustaining the regional organizing groups. They would pop up in other places, but then the energy would kind of deflate. There was a Life Center in Oregon briefly at one point, and there were strong networks in the Twin Cities and several other places, but Philadelphia was the only place where something at the level of a Life Center really developed.

We started out almost from the beginning with the Outreach Collective in Philadelphia that created brochures and literature, and answered inquiries from interested people. We also had newsletters. We had an outreach newsletter called the *Dandelion*—the idea being dandelions are things that just sort of pop up everywhere. We had an internal newsletter that was first called the *Dandelion Wine*, then abbreviated to the *Wine*, later called the *Grapevine*. The outreach newsletter was usually published in Philadelphia; the internal newsletter tried to rotate around the country, and had different collectives in different places take it on for a year or two. We also had directories of members. So those were the kind of things we had early on in terms of the glue, but it was still very minimal coordination.

That went on for a few years, and then the Outreach Collective morphed into something called the Network Service Collective. It continued to have those outreach functions, but was also seen as serving the needs of keeping the network together, because we realized we didn't really have much coordination and we needed more of that. So we tried to encourage and support the development of MNS local networks. We kept a mailing list up to date and tried to oversee the funding. We would have local network meetings once a month in Philadelphia, and those meetings worked pretty well. We'd decide to do something, and people would follow through. But on a national level, keeping the network together was always much shakier. Our real strength was Whole Network Meetings, gatherings where lots and lots of MNSers from all over the country would show up. The Whole Network Meetings were real energy builders and were where we attempted to make decisions.

In the early 1980s, having struggled with this whole coordination issue, we were more willing to have more coordination. But there was always this tension about leadership in MNS: "How do we do leadership and keep it democratic?" This was particularly difficult when we thought about coordination across the United States. First, we had a communication and coordination group that functioned with people from three clusters in three areas where MNS was most active: Philadelphia, the Twin Cities, and Tucson, Arizona. We would meet via speakerphone.

Then in 1984, we moved one step closer to a defined leadership structure. We developed the Network Coordinating Council that Betsy and I were a part of. By this time the problems with MNS were starting to show up, and we were trying to figure out what to do to move things forward. A man named Steve Chase, who was on the Network Coordinating Council, wrote something called the "Reorganizers Manual," which spelled out how we would need to organize ourselves if we wanted to be a cadre organization. After that, we wrote a more coherent *Organizational Handbook*. It was a good handbook [see "Documents" section below]. But by the time we got it done, we really were not in shape to use it. George talked about the difficulties of consensus getting in the way of changing. In some of the day-to-day small group activities, I think consensus worked fairly well. In terms of larger-scale decisions and trying to make major changes in organizational direction, it got in our way a lot.

Before I wrap up, I want to emphasize one great thing about the way MNS organized itself. Because we had this "bread labor" model, with people working roughly half time and devoting a lot of their time to political work, we were not paying organizers, so our fund-raising needs were minimal. We were not like a lot of the organizations out there now that are spending a huge amount of their time figuring out how to raise money. We did get some contributions to publish literature and those kinds of expenses. But we were never in the situation where we had to worry about the question, "If we do this politically, are we going to lose a chunk of funding that's going to cause big trouble?" And that was huge.

As I said at the outset, MNS was an experiment. We were trying to figure out how to coordinate a decentralized network of small groups and have it cohere in one direction. I think we still have a lot to learn about that.

Lynne Shivers

Shivers was a founding MNS member and active for nearly two decades in the Philadelphia Life Center. She is a college writing instructor and the coauthor of More Than the Troubles: A Common Sense View of the Northern Ireland Conflict *(New Society Publishers, 1985).*

For me, there are two main components that distinguished MNS and the community of the Life Center from most other organizations at the time. One was community living, and the other was nonviolence training. The first year we had three houses in the community in West Philadelphia. Eventually we had twenty houses. The other MNS founders and I caught on to the idea that community was important because the movement was terribly demoralized and many people were burned out. What we realized in the late 1960s was that many people were going to jail for various periods of time, and many people were experimenting with different ways of trying to move social change in the society. They were just working so hard and didn't figure out ways to support each other. Community was one way to try to do that.

Each house had its own unique name created by the people who lived there. The Stone House was the big stone building on Forty-Sixth Street just below Springfield Avenue. Then there was the Gathering, and Trollheim, and many others. The Youngest Daughter got its name from its residents throwing the I Ching! Most of the houses were mixed gender, but there was one house that had only women. There was one house that had only older people, and many houses had children as well. So the parents decided that they would figure out what kind of support and child care they wanted from the other members of the community. Then there would be negotiations between what the parents wanted and what the nonparents were willing to do. But few people moved out based on that issue.

The members of each house typically met weekly, sometimes for two or three hours. Personal check-ins always took place. The main part, of course, was the division of labor. If you have between six and eleven people in a house, you have a lot of work to be done: cooking, cleaning, food buying, cleaning up from meals, on and on and on. We made lists of fifteen or twenty jobs that had to be carried out weekly, and then we would change jobs every couple weeks or so. One of the things I liked about living in community is that we would usually pair ourselves up with somebody—for example, somebody who knew how to cook pretty well and somebody who didn't know how so well—so that there would be some learning going on there.

We also refined the idea of having support committees for members of the MNS community. Each person would choose people to be on his or her support committee. They could turn to the members of their committee when they were facing major decisions in their lives like "Should I take this job?" or "Should I move to Seattle?" I always made it a policy of choosing somebody who I knew did not know me well because I like the idea of somebody giving me brand-new insights. But support committees were also important for us in our personal lives, in things that were more intimate. I remember one member had surgery on the top of her spine, and there was a question of whether or not her legs would be completely paralyzed. So she asked her support committee to have at least one visitor stay with her all the time, even when she was sleeping, to hold her hand, because she felt that even if she wasn't conscious, her unconscious mind knew, and that physical connection was important to her.

A second element I want to talk about is training. It was a key component. We developed five different training programs to meet different needs. In the beginning, we had workshops for the residents of the houses and we created our own agenda. The words that I remember the most are "surviving and thriving in community." For almost all of us the community that we had created was brand new. We wanted to figure out what we were doing, and do it well. That training lasted for more than a couple months.

After a year or so, we began to get lots of visitors. They'd say, "Hi, I just came down from Boston and I want to find out what the Life Center is all about." If you were supposed to go to a meeting in an hour, and your job was to work up the co-op order and plan for the report you were going to give at the meeting, and this person wanted you to sit down and tell him or her about the Life Center, something wasn't going to work. This happened over and over again, and somebody got the brilliant idea to channel all these visitors into an orientation weekend. We gave them a taste of the macroanalysis seminars, of nonviolence training, of what it was like to live in community. On Sunday morning there was always a discussion on, "What are you going to do when you go home to help continue your work in social change?"

The second major training program was called the general training program, or GTP, which lasted for two weeks. That was scheduled five times a year, and was for learning the same skills, but taking more time for each element. It also included planning, executing, and evaluating a demonstration. In 1979, there was a movie playing downtown called *The China Syndrome*. It was the story of an explosion inside a nuclear power plant that in its worst scenario, seeped radioactivity through the earth into China. Life Center people had been leafleting outside and inside the movie theater about the fact that two nuclear power plants were being built in Limerick, outside Philadelphia, at that time. At the same time, the two-week training program had been planning to have a vigil outside the movie theater on Wednesday afternoon of the second week. Well, it poured cats and dogs. So they postponed it to Thursday morning, which was exactly the morning when the Three Mile Island accident took place. *LIFE* magazine came out and took photos of the little vigil outside the movie theater. It came out a couple weeks later, and movement groups around the country said, "Wow, the Life Center's really got it together! They were out there the first morning!" And we said, "Oh yeah, of course!"

The most ambitious of the training programs was the nine-month program, which we ran for about eleven years. Participants took part in a whole macroanalysis seminar, which lasted three or four months. As well, they were members of community houses, they learned a lot of skills, they were members of a collective, and they did co-op work like the rest of us. Finally there was a training that happened outside the Life Center, at the request of outside organizations. I remember, for example, Women Organized against Rape planned a march through Center City Philadelphia in the evening to point out places where women had been victimized and actually physically attacked. They asked me to train peacekeepers for that march, and I did, and it was a powerful demonstration.

I'll close with another example of the impact of training that sounds a little immodest, but in fact actually happened. A couple friends of mine went to Europe near the end of when European organizers were working against the placement of Cruise missiles in various countries. They asked the nonviolent action groups, "Where did your training come from, initially?" And all of them said, "The Life Center." To me, that's just a fabulous recognition of the impact and ripple effect of the work that we did there—that it grew. Where people saw the value of applying lessons to their own situations, they just went ahead and did it. And that's called a movement.

Robert A. Irwin

Irwin was active in MNS in Philadelphia and Boston from 1973 to 1988. He is the author of Building a Peace System *(Talman, 1989), and the "Revolution" entry in* Protest, Power, and Change *(Routledge, 1997), an encyclopedia of nonviolent struggle.*

I'm going to start by speaking a little bit about my personal experience of MNS. In my last year of college, I read an article in an obscure little radical magazine called *Win* [March 1, 1973 issue] that said in West Philadelphia, people were starting to find ways to do social change work together, but also to create a social base for it in which they could support each other. I thought, "Oh, this sounds really interesting. I can visit on spring break 'cause it's near my hometown." So I went to the address in the article, rang the doorbell at Stone House, and thereby became part of the motivation for the future MNS orientation weekends! The people were kind enough to find a way for me to have dinner with somebody, and then they said, "Go away, and in September we're going to have something organized that you can come to."

I came back in September and attended the first of the orientation weekends. You'd show up about dinnertime on Friday from wherever—which could be from another country, from around the United States, or locally—and there would be a dinner. Friday night we would all begin getting acquainted, learn the weekend's agenda, and the aims of MNS and its Philadelphia Life Center. Saturday morning we went through a "mini" version of the macro-analysis seminar process—a do-it-yourself method of group self-education, to make sense out of the bewildering chaos of multiple issues and develop a sense of what a group of people could do to make a dent in the problems where they lived. Then we would do a training exercise with some complex group dynamics lesson on Saturday afternoon. In the evening we'd have a party. On Sunday, we'd ask people to talk about how they could use what they'd learned back home, and try to talk people out of the idea of moving to the Philadelphia Life Center to enjoy all the good vibes and empowered feelings. The connections made during these weekends created new channels of energy. About three hundred people came to these weekends each year—over a decade, thousands.

At the orientation weekend, I heard there was going to be a training program for activists, so I applied and was accepted into that. Rather than sit back and be instructed, I found that by the second week, I was sitting down with George Willoughby, who had sailed into the Pacific Ocean nuclear test area in the 1950s to put his own body on the line against nuclear testing, and George was saying, "We don't believe in one-way hierarchy or stuff like that here. We're doing everything in an egalitarian and participatory way. So Bob, now it's up to us to develop a workshop on how to facilitate meetings effectively because that's one of the basic things that you're going to be doing a lot of when you're an activist. So what do you think?" I found out that it was, like, they throw you into the deep end of the pool! It was sort of a collective self-training, and in a few weeks the line between the collective that admitted us into the program and those of us who were new dissolved. In October someone said, "Bob, we need someone to coordinate these monthly orientation weekends. Why don't you coordinate the November one, and we'll have this other person work with you." I took my little handbook and started making phone calls, and I was coordinator of the November orientation weekend, which went off perfectly well. But again, this was a lesson in the tempo of learning in MNS. You do it in September; by late October you're in charge of the November version.

By the early 1980s, MNS began to let these crucial energy-mobilizing programs decline. I think this hurt the organization, but I want to discuss another issue that I think was even more of a problem. Oddly, MNS had no formal systematic method for internal education, or improvement of its analysis, vision, and strategy. Over time, MNS surely needed to update and deepen our understanding of the systems we were trying to transform. As groundwork for that, it seemed an uncontroversial plan to take certain items from our literature list and designate them as representing our "official" positions as an organization. It would be simple to designate some documents—which were already quite sensibly assumed by all outsiders to represent our positions—as a baseline from which to advance and refine our ideas. For example, how, if at all, should feminism modify the perspective in *Strategy for a Living Revolution* or *Moving toward a New Society*? The Macro-Analysis Collective that I belonged to proposed MNS do this.

When our proposal finally came up on the crowded agenda of the Whole Network Meeting, some saw little point to it—why formally agree to something we all already more or less agreed with?—and our argument seemed a bit abstract and hardly urgent to a good number of the meeting's participants. Finally, someone forcefully said: "We don't want to have a party line!" For an organization that would need to advance intellectually in a changing world— an organization that had nothing in common with the ugly Leninist-Stalinist tradition of top-down reversals of policy that the phrase party line evoked—such an assertion was demagogic. It was a bullet to the brain. Party line put an ugly label on a perfectly legitimate function: telling the public, and those in other organizations who might have allied with or joined us, where we stood. Amazingly, the remark effectively ended the discussion, killing the proposal. With consensus decision making, the status quo prevailed over change.

This decision—this nonchange and rejection of what was intended to allow us to evolve intelligently—was an early stumble toward the pattern that Andy diagnosed [earlier in this book]: "MNS had made little progress in bringing in new members and diversifying itself, due to the defining role that its own movement subculture played in the organization." If we did not define ourselves in a thoughtful, deliberate way, we would de facto define ourselves in another. No group offering guidance to society—guidance

away, that is, from militarism, sexism, racism, statism, imperialism, and environmental destruction, concepts designat-
ing complex realities that need to be understood in order
to be changed—can reasonably refuse the challenge to say
what it, as an organization, thinks about them. But by rejecting the formulating of an ever-clearer, more advanced
message to our fellow human beings, we began losing our
claim on their attention.

Finally, I want to respond to one aspect of Andrew's
claims about MNS. He makes two points I much agree
with, and one on which I must sharply differ. First, we
ought to learn from past experience and not repeat past
mistakes. Second, and more specifically, revolutionary
system transformation toward anarchist ideals cannot be
achieved through the proliferation of alternative institutions, no matter how exemplary.

Where I must differ is with his assertion that "MNS
strategy prioritized the creation of alternative institutions
that modeled egalitarian and anticapitalist values." We
never did that, and our first book [Lakey's *Strategy for a
Living Revolution*] specifically advocated a contrasting concept: counterinstitutions. George began by asking whether
certain "communes can be important in the sense that they
influence the culture by example." His response:

> Unfortunately, the strategy of change by exam-
> ple has most of its power muted by tolerance....
> Community self-help projects, like organizing new
> schools, . . . cooperative stores, and the like . . . all
> too often are a band-aid approach to a problem that

requires massive treatment. Neighborhood cooperative stores cannot challenge the corporate giants.
... The small structures are pitifully inappropriate
for challenging the increasing size of institutions
in Western industrial countries.... The cooperative store, neighborhood school, and so on are not
movement organizations, usually, but on the con-
trary tend to harden with success to become part of
the status quo. (ibid., 82–83)

Certainly this statement by a prominent founder of
MNS cannot be mistaken for prioritizing the creation of
alternative institutions or advocating "change by example."
It's closer to the opposite—and we never reversed this position. Andy mentions five efforts as illustrating what he sees
as MNS's emphasis on alternative institutions: a print shop
and a toy-making business, New Society Publishers, a food
cooperative, and a block association working to prevent
crime. His account continues, "Alternative institutions were
meant to demonstrate that radical activity could create
immediate, concrete improvements in people's lives." The
food co-op and crime prevention efforts fit this description.
For the others, it is a stretch to imply these showed people
that their lives could be improved by radical activity. Any
business selling something you want can improve your life.
Radical activity here blurs the distinction between an activity initiated or taken part in by self-identified radicals, and
activities intrinsically radical. To "attract neighbors" and
join in activities for mutual benefit is a good thing, but not
a strategy for revolution.

Nevertheless, it's true that some former MNS members believe "alternative institutions" were an important part of their work during those years. So what did MNS mean by counterinstitutions? Why didn't that term wholly displace alternative institutions, at least among MNSers? Unfortunately, counterinstitutions were defined only implicitly, seemingly as alternatives directly linked with oppositional political organizations or campaigns. Most explicitly, George wrote,

> When the self-help efforts take place in the *context* of a revolutionary movement, such as the Black Panthers' breakfast program or medical center, they take on a revolutionary character. To be more precise, counter-institutions become revolutionary when they:
> - Carry a revolutionary ideology,
> - Build a revolutionary organization,
> - Take place with the context of open revolutionary struggle. (ibid., 83)

Despite all these repetitions of "revolutionary," the remaining examples in this discussion of counterinstitutions are the constructive program of India's independence movement, and five institutions created by the United Farm Workers that supported their 1965 California grape strike and boycott—a drugstore, food co-op, service station, newspaper, and health clinic. These two large-scale campaigns won great victories, but neither was revolutionary by standard criteria. Large oppositional movements seem to have room for counterinstitutions, but revolutionary counterinstitutions are hard to find. If the MNS participants in the Clamshell Alliance had built, say, a photovoltaic or other kind of clean and safe power-generating plant across the street from the Seabrook nuke—construction site, I think that would have qualified as a counterinstitution. But it is hard to see how the circumstances of struggle (episodic mass actions) and economic requirements could have favored such a tactic.

Bill Moyer, another influential member of MNS, also had a position on alternative institutions worth describing. He argued that if you were going to have an alternative institution, and it had, say, five people involved, *one* of those five people should have the job solely of *spreading the idea* of the alternative institution. Like George, Bill thought that the status quo could absorb thousands of alternative institutions without fundamentally changing, but that presenting them explicitly as a challenge to the status quo could potentially help to overcome that limitation. "One of the five" was meant to make vividly concrete the crucial importance of that element. In practice, I don't know of any alternative institution that has given *that* high a priority to promoting its idea, compared to conducting necessary daily operations; thus, Bill was de facto rejecting alternative institutions as commonly found.

If challenged as to why he did not oppose the print shop and toy-making business being part of MNS, I speculate that he might have said that both provided a flexible livelihood for their members that enabled them to do a variety of worthwhile radical political activities that went beyond the functions of the alternative businesses. I know this was true of both collectives' members. That they could make a living doing something moderately progressive (e.g., making durable, noncorporate, imagination-friendly wooden toys) was preferable to my politically neutral job cleaning typewriters. Indeed, to my knowledge, in the course of MNS's history, counterinstitutions played no role, except by the loosest of definitions. Instead, alternative institutions played a positive role in our lives, but were peripheral to program and strategy.

To conclude, I want to emphasize that quite independently of the facts of what position MNS held, Andrew and I *agree entirely* on the importance of learning from the past, and the inadequacy of solely building alternative, or prefigurative, institutions as a strategy for social transformation.

Q&A with Former MNS Members

I'm wondering about MNS's initial generation. How did MNS get on its feet? What did its initial core look like? How did the training programs get started?

LAKEY: Well, just a hint or two on that. One is that some of the people who I most wanted to be part of MNS were strong personalities, and a few of them had been present in the creation of A Quaker Action Group in 1965. We used to have eight-hour meetings, and fight like cats and dogs. It was so hard to get things going, and I wasn't sure we could even do that again. Then there were new elements that were being brought in, including a couple people who served on Dr. King's national staff. One reason why the experience that I had in the Netherlands with the Shalom Network (which was also nurtured by a training center) really appealed to me was that in a sense, everybody could have their turf. So we could start this thing with a bunch of strong personalities, and Ross could say, "OK, I'll take on neighborhood safety." People could take their turf and gather people around them. From an idealistic point of view, that's maybe not the way we'd like to organize things, but it's pretty realistic in terms of human nature.

I do remember some times when people would say, "No blueprints, we're not going to have any blueprints." You know, that kind of antiblueprint thing. But even to get people in the same room to start an organization together, we did have to have some common principles. And that was the other important thing: we could agree that we needed a vision—we'd been trying long enough to make change without a vision that could inspire people toward a new society. So we did need to have some fundamentals of common analysis. And we did have to have some way of understanding how to get from here, our analysis, to there, our vision. At the same time, though, this would involve growing and changing. We can hash out our rough vision, provisionally. But by the time we get closer to that vision it will be in dialogue with other kinds of people who were not in the room. So it's not like we were in the British Museum figuring all this out. There's a dialogic process. Strategically, we're going to learn so much. But on the other hand, we can start from something. We can start from the legacy of the Wobblies and others. We have all these people we can learn from and stand on. It's silly to just be unstrategic because we're worried somebody's going to attack us. Hey, attack is part of it! So we needed to grow our trust of each other and also create the space to allow that dialogic process to happen.

IRWIN: MNS had a strong bias in favor of action and experimentation. You had to have the courage to go ahead and try something. I remember Bill Moyer saying, "Anytime you come up with an idea for a campaign, there are going to be people who give you forty-six reasons why it probably won't work." And he said, "What you have to do is to say, 'You may be absolutely right. And if we do this and it fails for those reasons, we'll come back and tell you that you were right. But we're going to go ahead and try to do it anyway.'" That's fundamental. You might fail. But try it. And learn from it.

You mentioned vision and the importance of visioning as a necessary part of forming any strategy and being revolutionary. I want to know how elaborate your vision was, how thought out it was, and was it written down? And what is it?

LAKEY: We wrote a book called *Moving toward a New Society*, where we challenged ourselves to devote one-third of the book to analysis, and another third to vision, chapter by chapter. So what kind of foreign policy do we want to see? What kind of economic system? What kind of cultural institutions? And then the last third of the book was on strategy. And we did it partly as a model. We thought, "Wouldn't it be wonderful if the incredible brainpower of people like [Noam] Chomsky was devoted not only to what's wrong but also to what's right, or what could be right?" I think we'd have so much more movement for social change if we were reaching for what we want instead of just constantly badgering ourselves with what we don't want.

IRWIN: I think it's extremely important to elaborate a vision. I'm somebody who says, "Hey, a blueprint isn't going to oppress me! Give me blueprints! Let me compare and improve blueprints. Don't tell me we'll improvise a whole new social order later!" In a sense, if you don't have a vision that you can argue is better than the status quo, then what are you being a big pain in the ass about? Why not just shut up and stop complaining?

I wanted to know about MNS's thinking about taking state power. Is it worth it, should it be done, should it not be done, can it be done, does it not have to be done? What was MNS's analysis of the state?

RAASCH-GILMAN: I really appreciate the question. You probably noticed when we were talking about what MNS did that we spent virtually no time on the political parties. And that was because in many ways our analysis of power suggested that power is at the grass roots, not at the top level. So it's not about taking over the state in order to have power. It's needing the power in order to make the state— if we have to have one at all—do the will of the people. I think that the focus of taking power away from the state was really about taking power at the grassroots level, and making sure that at the grass roots we have the ability and confidence to actually govern ourselves. Another thing that we talked about in MNS quite a bit was decentralization along bioregional lines. We talked about breaking up the United States in ways that would respect the economy and ecology of different parts of the United States.

LAKEY: One of the ways that I'm trying to learn more about that question is by studying Norway. It is Norwegian

peoples' experience of themselves—and I think it's valid—
that they are freer than a lot of people in the world. And
this is because they have so much control over their state.
Part of how they've gotten there is that once they took
state power, which was in 1935–36, the Germans came in
and then they had to do it again. So once they did it, they
didn't say to themselves, "Oh good, now we can relax."
They continued to struggle, struggle, struggle. The clear-
est example was fifteen years or so ago, when almost all the
leaderships of the national parties in Norway agreed that
they should join the common market, now the European
Union, and it appeared to be a done deal. But no, a grassroots movement insisted on a referendum and voted
against joining the European Union. There was a crisis of
confidence because nobody could be a government because they'd all been told, "You're totally off." So there was
this constitutional crisis for a while. And finally a caretaker
government came in, but with much more respect toward
the people. So that's an example of how I think democracy can keep redoing itself at least on a small scale, if the
people decide to keep struggling. Of course, it's only seven
million people.

One of the things I just can't believe is all those folks
who worked for [Barack] Obama, and then sat back and
said, "Now let him take care of it." With that attitude, no
people can maintain democracy. No people can maintain
democracy in any form as long as there is a dependency relationship created. "Let's put somebody in there, and then
he will then take care of us." That's us acting like five year
olds, needing the parents to take care of us. Norwegians

are maintaining democracy by not taking a five-year-old attitude toward leadership but instead saying, "We are still in charge." And as a result, their democracy is quite vital, and ours is quite corrupt and embarrassing.

It's really rare to find a synthesis on the contemporary Left of revolutionary action and also communalism, or community-based living. What were the tensions you experienced between activism and communalism? Did one outweigh the other? How did they influence each other? Were they one in the same thing, or were they two things that you put together?

RAASCH-GILMAN: Yes, the tension between the utopian and community aspect and the political action aspect was strong. I was often intolerant of the communal living aspect, the utopian aspect. To me, that aspect often seemed to take away from the concrete and forceful political action I wanted to see in the world. I say that, but I met my current partner in MNS. He was from the utopian wing, I'm from the "hard-bitten shop floor organizer" wing, and we've been together twenty-three years. We often say what holds us together is that we're like two wings of a bird, and that the breastbone is what unites us. MNS worked in the same way.

Can you discuss your thinking about MNS's role in gentrification in West Philadelphia? What was going on then, and what do you think the legacy of MNS is for the changing character of the neighborhood now?

LAKEY: During the yearlong organizing process, we looked at neighborhoods all over the city to try decide, "Where should we focus? Where should we build our community?" One reason for choosing this neighborhood is that it was planned to become a slum. White flight was to be stimulated. Already realtors were knocking on people's doors, saying, "The black people who are over on that side of Twenty-ninth Street are moving this way. You white home owner better sell now if you want to get any kind of decent price." And of course, "Sell your house through me!" This has happened in many neighborhoods in Philadelphia, of course. White people were stampeded out in order to turn the neighborhood over, which is how realtors make a lot of money. So one reason we chose this neighborhood was precisely because we wanted to do whatever we could to stabilize it so that it wouldn't become yet another Philadelphia slum but instead could become stably integrated racially.

One of the first things we had to do when we started building these houses was to create neighborhood institutions that would stabilize the neighborhood. The food co-op was extremely important. Even more important was the block safety program, because there were so many younger white couples who were poised—one foot in the suburbs already—to move out, and crime was one of their biggest issues. So we organized the block safety program in order to bring down the crime rate, in order to keep white people here, so that black people could integrate into a racially mixed neighborhood, rather than it be turned into another black slum owned, of course, by suburban people and realtors.

So our time was a time when we had a stably integrated neighborhood, both racially and class wise. Now that was a step toward what we now see as gentrification. And if the MNS was here now, I don't know what we would do, but I'm sure we would be involved in some way.

BRIGHAM: I was part of the group that bought the house now at 4811 Springfield Avenue, and we originally tried to buy a house on the 4800 block of Windsor Street. We had gone a fair amount of the way through the process, and the owner backed out of the sale. It turned out that there were a lot of current or ex-Philadelphia policemen living on that block, and they thought that we looked like the kind of people who might have black people over to our houses! So we bought the house at 4811 Springfield, and it became really clear to me in that process that the owners were white people trying to get out of the neighborhood.

I was fascinated to see the dynamics around the block safety program. We said that the way that the safety program would work is that we would commit to walking a certain block where people lived, provided they met once a month and had a block safety captain. So there was a minimum of an organization that we could connect to, there was training, and there was working together, always a team of people. Also, you're aware that there is a strong base of Catholic culture with the St. Francis Church a few blocks away. Very early on the church's school said, "We're happy if you to use our gym as a place for training." So that meant a neutral place, but also connected us with a very important organization in the neighborhood. It wasn't around the clock of course; it was from around eight to ten weekday nights. The police told us the crime rate went down in one year and they credited the block safety program. What self-respecting thief wants to have a witness to a break-in of a house?

The other comment to make is that within four to five years of the Life Center starting, a group of residents decided they had enough skills in fixing, painting, and repairs of houses that they wanted to offer that to neighborhood families cheaply, but still make some pocket money from that work. And that also developed into a way that the people could repair their houses and not move out.

Some of us were wondering how MNS interacted with the other groups that were around and doing work that overlapped in any way with MNS's work. If becoming a multicultural group was a big challenge, what were some of the ways that you tried to work on that challenge?

LAKEY: The community organizing that we did in West Philadelphia was extremely accordant with regard to race—the way we set up the block safety association, for example. We always had cochairs, an African American cochair and a white cochair. A lot of the block safety organizing involved classical community organizing—getting the neighbors in the living room, going through a conversation: "Do we really want more police? What have the police done for you lately? Do we really want our neighborhood to be a political base for Mayor [Frank] Rizzo to raise more money for police and put his police in this neighborhood when they don't really respond to our needs?" So we were developing all these great relationships with our neighbors and prospective neighbors, many of them African American. There were also African Americans in our group, but it was predominantly white.

The thing is that we were so intent on putting up front our radicalism—the counterculture dimension, not waiting until after the revolution to experiment with alternative kinds of relationships, for example. Men, actually together, sexually! Women actually together! We would walk down the street arm in arm. Anyway, sometimes people would say, "Why don't you just go into the countryside and do the farm thing, and nobody will pay attention? Why are you doing this in this Roman Catholic neighborhood? Why are you doing this in people's faces?" So it was this tricky line about, on the one hand, not trying to create animosity in the neighborhood so that we couldn't organize with the neighbors, and on the other, still being ourselves—still having a kind of integrity about our radicalness. That was one of the things that I hope you all can figure out better than we could, because we were just walking and dancing this line constantly.

NINA HUIZINGA: I was also involved in MNS in West Philadelphia. I'd like to bring up two examples. One has already been mentioned, which was the community organizing in this neighborhood. There were a lot of blacks and whites living in this neighborhood, and we organized block by block. Within the blocks, we worked together across racial lines, and there were times when there were tensions that came up that had to do with cultural things. But because we were organizing for a similar goal—everybody wanted to be safe—we managed to work together. And besides that, we all liked to eat cookies!

I also want to mention the "walk-in homesteads" because that's another time we crossed racial lines. There were about twenty different houses where people had walked into abandoned houses, invested their money to fix them up, and were facing eviction. I think the key that made that collaboration work is it was organized by black groups—one in North Philadelphia, and another in West Philadelphia. Denise Laws, who is black, had organized the folks in West Philadelphia. They held a meeting asking for the neighbors to support them in case of eviction. And I went with others from MNS.

On the day that the notice came down about eviction, it just so happened that I was giving a workshop on community organizing for MNS. So I just moved the location of the workshop to the house where they were being evicted. We ended up going inside the house before the police realized that we were there and helped the residents pack up to leave. Of course, we did it *very* carefully, and it took a *long* time! [*Laughter*] In the meantime, we were making telephone calls to all the different newspapers from inside the house. I was standing outside on the stoop explaining to everybody within earshot about why we have abandoned houses in Philadelphia, and why the idea of walking in and taking over the house was a good one.

The eleven of us, the "Chester 11," got arrested. It was Denise Laws, the organizer, three walk-in homesteaders, plus seven MNS types. We did a street demonstration in front of city hall on the day of the court hearing, and of the twenty houses, only two of them were successfully evicted. After that, we organized all the people who had walked into the homes—this was a black and white coalition by this time—and together we went down to negotiate with city hall. We were trying to get them included in a program that allowed people to keep abandoned houses if they could bring them up to code. We got that agreement, and we got this group that did cheap repairs involved in helping them do the necessary repairs. And eighteen of those twenty families kept their houses. That's a real victory!

The key, I think, is that the black organizations ran their own show. We were there in support of them. I think that is really, really important. It was much more useful than saying, "This is a white radical organization. Where are all the blacks? What's the problem with us?" I think we can accept who we are, and that we have a certain style that does or does not attract people cross-culturally. But there are organizations like Asian Americans United, for example, that are doing terrific work and would be glad to have support. They can be in charge of what they are doing, and we can show up to support.

Have you considered whether the emphasis on consensus and nonviolence was integral to the problem of MNS not being able to move beyond functioning as a white counterculture? Second, what do you make of the decline of nonviolence and consensus as part of broader movements?

IRWIN: There's no such decline regarding nonviolence. Also, I don't link nonviolence to white culture. I see nonviolent struggle as a technique used by groups that don't automatically have access to institutional power and have to find a way to mobilize power differently. Nonviolence is not a cultural limitation. It actually is one of the finer examples of human beings borrowing cross-culturally. Gandhi got ideas from the British suffragettes, from mass strikes in Russia, from boycotts in Ireland, even from a Chinese boycott of U.S. goods in retaliation against anti-Chinese racism in the United States. He combined militant tactics from anywhere with his own religious ideas and showed people ways to act effectively. That [idea] was picked up by Southern Baptist preachers and gay radical Quakers like Bayard Rustin, and it's spread to other cultures and places where people thought it couldn't work culturally. So it transcends any culture as a method of action. Gene Sharp's *Waging Nonviolent Struggle* [2005] has about twenty chapters updating his 1973 book about how it's been used in all kinds of cultural settings, including, believe it or not, Afghanistan. The Pashtuns, who are such fierce fighters, had a nonviolent movement in the 1920s and 1930s that was based on taking the militancy that was so prized in their culture, and turning it into nonviolent militancy. The excellent recent book on this, by Eknath Easwaran, is called *Nonviolent Soldier of Islam* [2nd ed., 1999], and there's even a film about it now [*The Frontier Gandhi: Badshah Khan, a Torch for Peace*, 2008].

RAASCH-GILMAN: In some of my experiences working with the RNC Welcoming Committee in the Twin Cities, planning for the 2008 [Republican National] Convention, I was a little surprised to see how consensus was being used. I would love to contribute to a more structured way of approaching consensus because it was my sense that it was getting in the way of making decisions—not because it was the wrong decision-making method, but because it lacked structure. I don't call that "decline," just "we could spruce this thing up a little bit." And just parenthetically, I also noticed how often groups seem to move toward consensus. They try to make decisions by consensus even if it's not what overtly they're doing; even if they think they're voting, they still are pushing toward making decisions by consensus. All kinds of groups do that.

Regarding the decline of nonviolence, I don't agree with that analysis either. I think that within the United States, we have gotten used to using the same nonviolent tactics over and over and over again, and have gotten very repetitious and are not particularly strategic. In the United States we do the same little pattern of rallies, marches, leafleting, and witnessing, which are fine tactics, but we're lacking an edginess. We aren't as innovative as we really need to be, and as we used to be. People in other parts of the world are much more innovative with nonviolent tactics at this point. I was personally really inspired by the Gaza Freedom March, in January 2010, which seemed like it was militant, dedicated, and creatively decentralized.

LAKEY: I just quickly would like to agree with regard to class in relation to consensus. I do think that culturally, working-class people—I'm working class myself—are more likely to get impatient with the amount of time that consensus characteristically takes than middle-class people are. And so I think organizations that decide they want to do consensus need to do a little class analysis as they make that decision, and raise that question as one consideration: "Are we going to limit ourselves in terms of our class base if we insist on consensus?"

I have a question about strategy. I'll just go out on a limb and say this: I think that we're lacking strategy and a collective way to produce it. So I wanted to hear from you all about how you saw building people's organizations as being part of a way of also building strategy collectively. When I say strategy, I mean revolutionary strategy: How are we going to make revolution in our lifetimes, if that's possible? It seems like you all took that seriously. Now we're here in West Philly, left with the legacies of these institutions that were started and built by MNS—the houses, the co-op, these things—and I wonder, "What are we using these spaces for in a strategic way?"

RAASCH-GILMAN: I just love this question. Thank you so much for asking it. I don't think we are going to be able to answer it adequately in the few minutes we have. But I think the most important thing is to affirm the need for constantly developing, articulating, evaluating, and refining strategy. However, one of the takeaways from MNS was something called *The Movement Action Plan*, written by Bill Moyer.[1] *The Movement Action Plan* is a helpful tool for strategizing, because Bill used his experience to show how movements actually develop and how they follow their own patterns.

LAKEY: The old tradition about strategy, including for Gandhi, unfortunately, was go off to the ashram, figure something out, come back and tell us what to do. But the beauty about the tools that have been developed since the 1990s is that they are about the group itself figuring out what to do, but in a more creative way because of the assistance of those tools. One reason for starting Training for Change in the early 1990s is that it seemed that we'd taken a giant step in MNS in terms of training skills and process skills, but that there was way more to develop. So we started Training for Change as a venue in which we could develop more skills, especially how to work democratically with groups so that they can evolve their own strategies—strategies that are not just repetitions of things that are already out there but that are organic to the group and its situation, and also are far-reaching, so that we're really talking seriously about transformation or revolution.

I'm going to say, as a way of leaving, that I totally appreciate what folks have said and the thoughtfulness you've shown. I have this confidence welling up in me now that when you organize your equivalent, if you do, of MNS, it will be better than ours.

DOCUMENTS

Why Nonviolence?

The present state of the people's movement against nuclear power and nuclear weapons is exciting and promising. The spread of groups using nonviolent direct action has demonstrated how wide and deep is the opposition to deadly nuclear technology and the priorities and needs of the ruling power structure. The development of nonviolent direct action campaigns as a principal means of struggle has greatly expanded the ranks of those taking an active and committed part.

For many people, nonviolence remains mysterious, controversial, or both. This paper provides a short introduction to nonviolent struggle and to some of its contemporary applications, so as to help dispel some of the mystery and clarify the controversies....

Why Nonviolence? was written by Bob Irwin and Gordon Faison in 1978. MNS distributed over a hundred thousand copies throughout the country in the wake of the successful Seabrook antinuclear power campaign. A full version of the essay, updated by Irwin in 1983, is available at http://www.vernalproject.org/papers/understanding/WhyNV/WhyNonviolence.html.

History, Methods, and Varieties of Nonviolence

Nonviolent action is a means of social struggle that has begun to be developed in a conscious way only in the last several decades. It does not rely on the goodwill of the opponent but instead is designed to work in the face of determined opposition or violent repression. It is not limited to any race, nationality, social class, or gender, and has been used successfully in widely varying political circumstances.

Nonviolent action is not simply any method of action that is not violent. Broadly speaking, it means taking action that goes beyond normal institutionalized political methods (voting, lobbying, letter writing, verbal expression) without injuring opponents. Nonviolent action, like war, is a means of waging conflict. It requires a willingness to take risks and bear suffering without retaliation. On the most fundamental level, it is a means by which people discover their social power. . . .

Gandhi's Pioneering Contribution

The career of Mohandas Gandhi (1869–1948) marked a watershed in the development of nonviolent struggle. In leading the struggle for Indian independence, Gandhi was the first to combine a variety of tactics according to a strategic plan in a campaign of explicitly nonviolent action, and the first to conduct a series of campaigns toward long-term goals. Deeply religious, practical, and experimental in temperament, Gandhi was a shrewd, tireless, and efficient organizer who united cheerfulness with unshakable determination. He was not only a political strategist but a social visionary. Gandhi's nonviolence had three main elements: 1) self-improvement (the effort to make oneself a better person), 2) "constructive program" (concrete work to create the new social order aimed at), and 3) campaigns of resistance against evils that blocked the way forward, such as the caste system and British colonial exploitation. Gandhi's success in linking mass action with nonviolent discipline showed the enormous social power this form of struggle could generate. While his contribution was overwhelmingly positive, it is also true that his experimental, unsystematic approach and personal charisma make it difficult to disentangle those aspects of his approach peculiar to Indian society, or which expressed his personal eccentricities, from those aspects of nonviolent action of possible universal application. . . .

It is through nonviolent direct action campaigns in the tradition of Gandhi that most people in the United States have become aware of nonviolence and nonviolent methods. In fact, despite the many violent aspects of American history of which we have become increasingly aware in recent years, the United States has its own native tradition of nonviolence. Staughton Lynd has noted that "America has more often been the teacher than the student of the nonviolent ideal" (*Nonviolence in America*). . . .

"Pacifism is necessarily revolutionary," wrote Paul Goodman in 1962. "We will not have peace unless there is a profound change in social structure." But this conclusion has by no means been obvious to everyone—or at least, most pacifists have shied away from the size of the task it implies. Perhaps the chief pioneer of revolutionary nonviolence in America was A. J. Muste (1885–1967: pronounced MUS-tee), whose early position can be found in a 1928 article titled "Pacifism and Class War." Muste, a minister who had lost his job for opposing World War I, had become an important leader of labor struggles. He demanded of pacifists who were critical of the violence in some labor actions that they recognize "the violence on which the present system is based. . . . So long as we are not dealing honestly and adequately with this 90 percent of our problem, there is something ludicrous, and perhaps hypocritical, about our concern over the 10 percent of violence employed by the rebels against oppression . . . . In a world built on violence, one must be a revolutionary before one can be a pacifist." On such grounds, for a time he turned away from pacifism; he and his followers played a major role in organizing the unemployed, and he was for a time a highly regarded ally of the Trotskyist movement. But he became convinced through experience of the inadequacy of Marxism-Leninism, and sought a politics that would be simultaneously revolutionary and nonviolent.

A concise expression of such a politics, surprisingly contemporary in tone, came in 1945 from the Committee for Nonviolent Revolution:

> We favor decentralized, democratic socialism guaranteeing worker-consumer control of industries, utilities, and other economic enterprises. We believe that the workers themselves should take steps

to seize control of factories, mines, and shops. . . .
We advocate such methods of group resistance as
demonstrations, strikes, organized civil disobedience, and underground organization where necessary. We see nonviolence as a principle as well as a
technique. In all action we renounce the methods
of punishing, hating or killing any fellow human
beings. We believe that nonviolence includes such
methods as sit-down strikes and seizure of plants.
We believe that revolutionary changes can only occur through direct action by the rank and file, and
not by deals or reformist proposals. . . .

As a basis for organized political actions, such ideas at
that time involved at most a few dozen people. Yet through
Liberation magazine, founded by Muste in 1956 with the
aid of the War Resisters League, and under the creative edi-
torial care of Dave Dellinger, Barbara Deming, Sidney Lens,
Staughton Lynd, and others, a new nonviolent, libertarian
socialism began to develop. Muste and later Dellinger were
able, owing to their trustworthy reputations and principled
independent radical stance, to play key roles in the various
coalitions of pacifist, Left, and other elements coordinating
mass actions against the Vietnam War from 1965 onward. . . .

But it was the movement of black people for civil
rights and an end to racial oppression that imprinted the
idea of nonviolence on the American consciousness. . . .
King's important role as a spokesperson and moral sym-
bol of the struggle has frequently led to an underemphasis
of the grassroots, decentralized nature of the movement,

whose heart was the decision by thousands of people to risk their security and often their lives on behalf of the cause, and to grow toward a greater fulfillment of their own potential in pursuit of justice and human community.

The civil rights movement had enormous and lasting impact. It affected both blacks and whites through the legal and institutional changes it brought, and it also created a body of people with a shared moral and political background from which they could move on to challenge other injustices like the Vietnam War, imperialism, poverty, and sexism. This achievement was often minimized by those who became increasingly radicalized by their experience when they saw clearly how much more remained to be done— that they were engaged in more than correcting a flaw in an otherwise-healthy system. Those entering the movement for social change later sometimes took for granted the gains that had been made at such cost. . . . Although the civil rights movement and Dr. King were moving into wider arenas, the experience can still serve as a reminder of the limitations of a nonviolent movement focusing on a single issue, be it war or racism, rather than aiming at the revolutionary transformation of the whole society. . . .

Nonviolent revolutionaries arising from the experience of the 1960s and early 1970s continue many the emphases of the earlier nonviolent movements. As we work to replace capitalism, we strive to change ourselves in ways that eliminate the role our own personal behavior plays in perpetuating sex, race, class, and other oppressions. We reject the capitalist conception of "the good life" based on compulsive consuming in favor of a richer way of life grounded in higher self-awareness, fun, and more social satisfactions—a way of life fully realizable for all only through revolutionary change. We espouse nonhierarchical organization and consensus decision making. We are seeking better ways to "empower" people through training programs (including group dynamics and peer counseling) and workshops; and by developing skill-sharing manuals we are attempting to multiply sources of initiative in the movement. Our political work includes educational efforts to spread an analysis of society, a vision of a better one, a strategy for getting from here to there, and the organizing of nonviolent campaigns as part of that strategy.

The Spreading of Antinuclear Campaigns

Before discussing the theory and dynamics of nonviolent action, it is useful to consider how the adoption of nonviolent direct action as a method of struggle often occurs. Despite the important role adherents of some type of principled nonviolence often play, most instances of mass nonviolent struggles are not initiated by them. "The major advances in nonviolence have not come from people who have approached nonviolence as an end in itself, but from persons who were passionately striving to free themselves from social injustice" (Dave Dellinger, "The Future of Nonviolence"). The typical structural conditions leading people to resort to nonviolent struggle are that more conventional political and legal channels appear blocked, yet people are unwilling to abandon their goals, as was so clearly the case in the struggle against nuclear power. Out of their own creativity or, more often, through hearing of or remembering events that seem relevant, people discover a way to act.

This process, however, need not be spontaneous; it can be deliberately fostered. In a 1972 speech titled "De-developing the U.S. through Nonviolence," MNS co-founder William Moyer proposed a strategy for a nation-wide and transnational movement against nuclear power. Rather than starting by forming a national coalition of sponsoring groups (a process with several disadvantages detailed in the article),

> The campaign-movement approach encourages groups to organize whatever local socio-dramas they believe to be creative and important. Small groups begin small projects in different places, joining others only when interests coincide. The key here is not the size of initial numbers but the ability to organize a local campaign with drama, crises, and other socio-dramatic elements. Even when all these ingredients are present, however, there is no guarantee that a project will take off into a full-fledged movement. The strategy of the campaign-movement approach to nationwide ef-forts is that if enough independent socio-drama projects are begun, there will soon be one that reaches a takeoff point, with much drama, crisis, publicity, and interest.

This, of course, is precisely what happened in the worldwide struggle against nuclear weapons and other social movements.

The Dynamics of Nonviolent Action

The conventional view of power is that it is something some people have and others don't. Power resides in soldiers, authority, ownership of wealth, and institutions. The nonviolent theory of power is essentially different: rather than seeing power as something possessed, it argues that power is a dynamic social relation. Power depends on continuing obedience. When people refuse to obey rulers, the rulers' power begins to crumble. This basic truth is in a sense obvious, yet it took the dramatic historical episodes of Gandhi's civil disobedience campaigns to begin to establish a new model of power. In routine social life this truth is obscured, but events like Seabrook cannot be understood without it.

From the standpoint of the conventional theory of power, what happened at Seabrook in April–May 1977? Protesters came and occupied a dusty parking lot; they were arrested and taken away. Action and reaction. Beginning and end. Defeat—they were all in jail. In reality the picture was far more complex. Instead of two social actors at work—the Clamshell Alliance and Governor [Meldrim] Thomson of New Hampshire—a whole range of intermediary forces was involved. Nonviolent action has significant effects on these forces, in ways we will describe, using

Seabrook as our model. Gene Sharp's later chapter titles in *The Politics of Nonviolent Action* provide a convenient outline: laying the groundwork for nonviolent action; challenge brings repression; solidarity and discipline to fight repression; and ways that success may be achieved.

Laying the groundwork is fundamentally important. This means defining goals and objectives, choosing strategy and tactics, making contingency plans, training, etc. Nonviolence is not magic; it is a way of mobilizing the strength we have for maximum effectiveness. In the outline above we see that the "action and reaction" that seemed to be the whole story are only the beginning. Along with the leading actors who clash with each other, there are also Clamshell members who are not committing civil disobedience but playing active support roles; potential participants who didn't feel enough urgency or sense of being needed to take part in the particular action; people who would like to see an end to nuclear power but don't plan to do anything about it; people oblivious to the issue; people hostile to "environmentalists who delay needed progress"; people who say "lawbreakers should be punished," but will limit themselves to griping; on down to utility executives, the governor's staff, bank presidents, etc. There are also police and perhaps National Guardspeople whose job it is to counter the demonstrators, but whose personal attitudes may lie anywhere on the spectrum.

The actions of the main social actors potentially affect all these people. The outbreak of conflict draws attention to the issue. In an important respect the two sides are not fighting each other directly but also competing with each other for the support of the public. On an issue like nuclear power, where there are many reasons to be against it and where opposition is growing, almost any public discussion favors antinuclear forces. When nonviolent direct action has been initiated, pronuclear forces often try to portray the activists as a small, irresponsible group that is flouting the public interest. (This image in fact, however, fits the pronuke forces all too readily!) A next step can be to invoke general principles like obedience to law to stir fears of disorder. But well-disciplined nonviolent action works against this diversion. Openly friendly and orderly activists pose little apparent threat to the public; with the onset of repression the question tends to arise, Why did they put themselves in such personal jeopardy? Is the repression justified? If their behavior can be made to serve their cause in this way, the activists may be on the road to success. Attempts to distort the image of the activists may fail and backfire; e.g., when one of the best-organized nonviolent actions in history is described as the work of "terrorists," even the unsympathetic are likely to raise a skeptical eyebrow.

To gain their desired result, agents of repression must make the activists lose their solidarity and abandon their goals. If they maintain solidarity and discipline, repression becomes ineffective. But solidarity alone does not bring success. That may come through a kind of "political jujitsu," in which the repressive efforts themselves tend to shift the balance of power toward the nonviolent activists. People on the side of the activists increase their level of involvement, while those allied with the oppressive power may reduce their support or switch sides. Shifts of attitude are important as well as shifts of behavior, because both sides adjust their actions according to how they gauge their support. Costly incarceration posed a question to New Hampshire residents—"Is it worth it?"—a question to which they were bound to answer "no" before long.

Nonviolent action is not dependent on the opponent's being repressive or making mistakes. It is not stymied when the opponent is moderate and conciliatory. Most of the methods mobilize political strength regardless of the opponent's response.

This brings us to the question of how nonviolent action may attain its goals. Three main ways have been identified: conversion, accommodation, and nonviolent coercion. Conversion means that the opponent has a change of heart or mind, and comes to agree with and work toward the activists' goal. At the top of the social structure, this is fairly unlikely, but significant instances may occur: for example, Daniel Ellsberg, who released the Pentagon Papers after being converted to opposition to the Vietnam War; Bob Aldridge, who left his job as chief missile designer for the Trident submarine in order to speak out against the growing threat of nuclear catastrophe.

At the other extreme is nonviolent coercion, where the activists have it directly in their power to frustrate the opponent's will. One example is the refusal by all workers to work on a construction project that a union has declared unecological (Australia's "green bans"); another was the invention of the "search-and-avoid" missions by GIs in Vietnam who did not want to risk their lives in an unpopular war. Most commonly, the outcome is determined by an intermediate process.

Accommodation means that the opponents give in, partly or completely, not because they have changed their minds, and not because they are completely powerless, but because it seems a lesser evil than any other alternative. It may be because continuing the struggle at that point would probably mean further erosion of support. Concessions may also be granted to halt the consciousness-raising process of struggle that would lead people to discover how much power they really have. . . .

Organizational Handbook

Section 1: Purpose

A. Why an Organization?

There is some appeal in the seemingly total "freedom" of the unaffiliated individual activist who can work at her/his own pace or switch projects at will; spends no time on "internal" organizational matters; and feels free of responsibility for the defects of all the flawed organizations working for social change.

But such an activist's ability to achieve her/his goals is continually constrained: by the lack of a nurturing community of coworkers with shared assumptions and ideals; by a

---

This passage is from the final MNS *Organizational Handbook*, prepared by the Network Coordinating Committee and adopted in 1986. These selections provide a useful summary of the conclusions regarding organizational structure and political leadership arrived at by MNS after fifteen years of action and reflection.

lack of criticism and encouragement; by the inability to allocate sizable resources to the development of new activists; new ideas, and useful literature; and by the lack of U.S.-wide and transnational programs and priorities. The feeling of powerlessness that unaffiliated individuals sometimes experience is rooted in the reality of the limitations of uncoordinated efforts.

We know that there are many kinds of work to be done in building a movement for social change. No one of us, or even one local group, can do it all. We can maximize our influence and feel more effective through strong connections to people across the country and around the world who are working toward the same goals. These connections affect how we see ourselves and our work, and build our morale.

To join MNS is to choose to exchange the frustrated "freedom" of the unaffiliated activist for the different constraints and expanded capabilities of organized political effort. Participation in MNS is for individuals who understand the value of an organization that coordinates activities. Activists in MNS want their work strengthened in this way and want it combined with the activity of others into a whole that is, through synergy, greater than its parts.

B. Why a Broader Network?

MNS is the only U.S.-wide organization explicitly advocating nonviolent revolution. The ideas of revolutionary nonviolence have been developing for at least thirty years in the United States and elsewhere, although revolutionary nonviolence is not yet highly visible as an alternative to the approaches of violent revolution or change through the normal channels of the system.

We believe that a U.S.-wide organization with a movement-building strategy can have significant impact in developing the ideas of revolutionary nonviolence. It also can influence others to learn more about this way of creating change and to consider it as a serious possibility. In 1982, we made a commitment to develop MNS as a strong movement-building organization that coordinates its efforts on local, regional, and U.S.-wide levels and maintains strong transnational ties.

Our primary day-to-day work will be direct participation in social change efforts and resource sharing in our local communities. Given our vision of a decentralized society, much of our work on developing new alternatives will be done on the local and regional levels. However, we recognize that because economic, political, and military power is heavily concentrated at the national and even transnational levels (e.g., multinational corporations), we need the organizational capability to struggle at those levels, to move in a unified direction, and to take unified action when appropriate. As a U.S.-wide organization, we need to be able to work with other activists and organizations to generate enough power to create social change. Our combined local efforts must constitute a movement powerful enough to affect the entire United States.

The resources we can bring to bear as a U.S.-wide organization strengthen the work done by our members in local areas, and increase our ability to spread our ideas in the wider movement and beyond. We exchange information about our work, learn from each other's successes and mistakes, and provide each other with new ideas and inspiration. Our varied experiences and perspectives contribute to the continuing development of our analysis and strategy. We provide ongoing support, share resources, and help each other in times of crisis—all important for sustaining us as we move against the mainstream. We provide resources that can't be provided effectively by any one local organization (e.g., literature and study guides). We facilitate travel of MNS members as speakers and trainers. The ability to bring outside resources to local areas is especially important to MNS members and sympathetic activists in areas without local MNS organizations.

Ultimately, to increase our influence, MNS needs to organize and work in many more local areas. Outreach brochures, the New Society Packet, and the outreach newsletter, all produced by the whole network, help new people learn about MNS. Key functions of our network are to maintain contact with people in isolated areas, support the organizing and development of new locals, provide ongoing nurturance to locals, and assist locals experiencing difficulty. The network also provides the potential for building organizational coherence by developing a means for local accountability to the whole.

As a revolutionary organization, our goals are ambitious and our tasks many. Even with steady growth, we must choose wisely among many possible directions for our social change work. We must continue to develop strategies that take into account issues of power and influence on the global level. Such choices and strategies require leadership and thinking beyond the local or regional level. The U.S.-wide organization cannot replace local initiative or strategy but it can provide a larger context for such efforts and a coherent overall strategy for large-scale social change.

We value and want to continue our tradition of local autonomy, decentralization, and participatory democracy, combined with discipline and joint planning at all levels. We do not want to be a centralized, bureaucratic, top-down organization that detracts from local and regional efforts. We believe that the resources, energy, and potential power of a well-organized and geographically dispersed network can be a vital asset to, rather than a drain on, local and regional organizing. Some general organizational and co-ordination functions are best handled at the networkwide level. However, the networkwide organization should not absorb functions that can be productively filled at the local or regional level.

As we experiment with building a large-scale, participatory, democratic, nonhierarchical organization with appropriate functions at appropriate levels, we provide organizations everywhere with an alternative organizational model. . . .

Section 3: Self-governance

A. Empowerment

MNS is an experiment in organizing. Because our organization evolves and changes as we try new agreements and processes, it incorporates the results of many members' thinking and review. The results of our pooled action and reflection are contained in this handbook.

Our political actions are based on a strategy for social change that involves personal growth, cultural preparation, organization building, and agitating for revolutionary reforms. We encourage each member to envision a just society that takes into account the well-being of people and the planet, then to work with other activists to bring this new society into being. To achieve our goals, we rely heavily on the empowerment of ourselves and others. We bring the principle of empowerment to bear on our own organization as well. What we have created and are creating is in so many ways different from what we see around us that we have given it a name: "empowerment organization."

Past experience has taught us that the way in which we organize our work has a strong influence on how we feel and what we accomplish. Typically, when people join together to work on a common project, they choose (or allow someone to dictate) either a boss-directed way of working (authoritarian) or a no-boss way of working (informal and spontaneous). Both ways of organizing work have strengths and weaknesses. People who become bosses or managers take some greater share of responsibility for leadership, which may contribute to getting the job done on time. However, the boss/person is only human, and sooner or later may get overwhelmed with demands, or too greedy for influence. When this happens, the person's ability to lead is hurt.

At the same time, the people who work for a boss often lose their own power to initiate or take responsibility for the progress or nature of the work. As workers, we learn to keep our mouths shut in front of higher-ups and do our griping out back, with no effect. Even when we choose to organize in friendly, informal small groups without a chosen leader, these roles and responses are likely to surface. "Leaderless" groups often are limited in their effectiveness. Members of such groups may have such a strong reaction against "authority" that they will unthinkingly attack any member's attempt to take initiative.

Both boss-directed and no-boss groups are based on a worldview that says there is only a limited amount of power. Both lead to competition for this supposedly scarce resource. In our view, power is a personal attribute that can be pooled in cooperative efforts, used to manipulate other people or things, given away to others, demonstrated in acts of nonviolent resistance, and much more. When we come up against an inability to get things done, we choose to cooperate with each other to find more power, rather than to compete with each other for what little there appears to be. If that doesn't work, we try to share what we have equally, rather than eye suspiciously anyone who seems to have more.

As members of an empowerment organization, people in MNS seek to behave and organize work in ways that respect and protect each person's unique ability to think and act creatively. We are committed to mutual aid, shared experience, and nonviolent direct action. We bring into our lives today what we would like our children to inherit tomorrow.

Empowerment organization is a model for a new society, neither authoritarian nor spontaneous. It requires from each of us a great deal of self-discipline, cooperation, and love. The following principles guide us.

B. Principles of Self-management

Since MNS was founded, people have learned a great deal about what works (or doesn't) in organizations. Students of workplace democracy and the successful maintenance of democratic, participatory structures and functioning have identified the following principles as essential.

1. PARTICIPATION IN DECISION MAKING, EITHER DIRECTLY OR BY SELECTED REPRESENTATION THAT REFLECTS CONCERNED GROUPS

MNS puts great stress on participation, which occurs face-to-face at meetings, through written and oral communications, and through choosing people to whom specific decision-making responsibilities are delegated. We emphasize consensus decision making in face-to-face meetings. No decision-making method always combines every element we want: participation, efficiency, economy, speed, commitment, and wisdom. We continue to study and experiment with the suitability of different functions: face-to-face decision making, conference phone calls, consensus, and other forms of decision making.

2. FREQUENT FEEDBACK OF RESULTS TO ALL MEMBERS

Reports at local, regional, and networkwide MNS meetings, in MNS task and support groups, and in our newsletters and publications help us to monitor the results of our work. Although some of the most important social change work is hard to measure (such as changes in consciousness that do not show up in action until years later), we are seeking better ways to specify and evaluate the results we aim for and actually produce. We recognize that reporting and evaluating our work—successful, unsuccessful, or mixed—both to our membership and to wider audiences, are important uses of our organizational resources.

3. FULL SHARING OF KEY ORGANIZATIONAL INFORMATION AND, TO THE EXTENT POSSIBLE, KEY ORGANIZATIONAL EXPERTISE

For MNS, this means both the feedback of results just mentioned and much more: information on our membership and finances; organizational conflicts and issues; the capabilities of individuals and groups in the MNS; a bird's-eye view of the state of the whole organization; and finally, the state of the world, our country, public moods, events, trends, the plans and activities of our allies and opposing political forces, etc. The gathering of this scattered information and its sifting, analysis, and presentation in useful form are major challenges for all individuals and organizations working for social transformation.

4. AGREED-ON INDIVIDUAL RIGHTS (RECOGNIZING INDIVIDUAL DIFFERENCES)

5. METHODS OF CONFLICT RESOLUTION AND MEDIATION IN CASE OF DISPUTES, USING MEDIATORS CHOSEN AND AGREED ON BY THOSE INVOLVED

6. A PARTICULAR SET OF VALUES AND ATTITUDES (A TYPE OF CONSCIOUSNESS), INCLUDING A WILLINGNESS TO ENGAGE IN MUTUAL AID, RESISTANCE TO BEING MANIPULATED, AND ENCOURAGEMENT TO CREATE AND ORGANIZE AROUND COMMON GOALS

These are sought both in the structure and in the "spirit," "ethos," or "organizational culture" of MNS. They grow in our own characters as we formally train and informally resocialize ourselves in the course of our political work and organizational life. We maintain them by striving constantly to exemplify "empowering" behavior.

7. SYSTEMS AND PRACTICES FOR MAINTAINING AND ENHANCING DEMOCRATIC STRUCTURE AND FUNCTIONING, INCLUDING WRITTEN DESCRIPTIONS OF THE RESPONSIBILITIES OF ALL ROLES IN THE ORGANIZATION, FORMAL TRAINING, AND OTHER PRACTICES

This handbook reflects our growing appreciation of the importance of practices and systems that nurture shared power. Our organizational structure and functioning often will embody careful innovation, learning, and creative thought, making them unfamiliar and not immediately understandable; but they should be explicit and clear enough to be understood by a prospective member willing to study our *Organizational Handbook* and related documents.

8. EXPLICIT RECOGNITION OF HOW WE LEARN AS AN ORGANIZATION AND CREATION OF ADDITIONAL ORGANIZATIONAL LEARNING OPPORTUNITIES, WHERE NEEDED

It is important that an organization have effective ways to communicate information and insights, and to surface problems and debate issues. Without such an ability, it may slide toward undemocratic practices or cling to ineffective ones. As any organization evolves within its changing environment, it requires ways to evaluate its experience and to focus special attention on its own health. This may require reform or redesign of existing systems. Group retreats, self-study, special task forces, consultation with outside experts, regular evaluation times at meetings, informal discussions, and other means may be used to serve these purposes, and in general to assess whether MNS is indeed doing its best to help move humankind toward a "new society."

This list of principles almost certainly will be elaborated, simplified, or otherwise changed as our understanding and experience grow. It guides us in deciding organizational practices.

C. Leadership

Leadership is a word that carries a heavy load. Centuries of rule by men over women, the wealthy over the poor, and light-skinned people over dark-skinned people have made the meaning of leadership seem the same as "domination" by a "ruler" over lowly subjects.

In groups of people who are organizing against the injustice of such "rule," there is a natural distrust of any one person becoming too powerful. Rather than working to share power, people get tangled up in conflicts about who has power and who doesn't. The fights that get started in this way have kept many groups from success in challenging the injustices that brought them together.

In MNS, leadership is a quality we want to encourage in each other. We look for ways to share the power and influence that come from taking the risks of leadership as well as the learning that comes from mistakes. We view leadership as a range of skills: most of us have some skills, all of us can learn most skills, and no one person needs all skills. We promote a democratic and participatory, rather than paternalistic or autocratic, leadership style. In this way, everyone develops the capability to perform at least several of the functions of leadership, such as initiating, seeking information or opinions, giving information or opinions, clarifying, summarizing, testing for consensus, reducing tension, exploring differences, encouraging, compromising, and listening to feelings.

We have developed many structures and ways of doing things to encourage and support the involvement of everyone in the functions of leadership. In this way, rather than insisting that everyone be alike in their powerlessness, or that one person shoulder most of the load, we encourage the empowerment of all. "Shared leadership" is a term we use to describe this.

CONCLUSION

MNS and the Current Moment

This book arrives at a strange and difficult political moment. Social and economic crises continue to pile up, but in the U.S. at least, movements seeking liberatory solutions to these crises remain dispersed and relatively weak. Instead, the fear and resentment felt by millions of U.S. Americans have been successfully parlayed into the right-wing populist Tea Party movement.[1] In Greece, Italy, and other parts of Europe, austerity measures and other attempts to resolve the crisis of financial capitalism on the backs of students, workers, and immigrant communities have been met with much more concerted and visible resistance. Images of rowdy occupations of university buildings, mass demonstrations, and attacks on the British royal motorcade circulate instantly online, inspiring envy among leftists in North America. We are also witnessing an outpouring of new radical theory, as European philosophers seek to reinvent communism, South American indigenous communities assert their autonomy from traditional state structures, and a panopoly of strategic paths to revolutionary transformation have been reconsidered and refashioned.[2] This creates a situation in which imitation—the straightforward transplanting of tactics—and voluntarism—the feeling that it is possible to will a revolutionary situation into existence—become enormously tempting, despite the different political environments and policing regimes we find ourselves living in.

So what use is it to study MNS—or other radical initiatives of the past, for that matter—at a time like this? MNS's ideas don't offer any magic bullets. I do believe, however, that examining the specific experiences of an organization that shared many of the investments and beliefs of contemporary radicals can help point toward ways of moving past current stumbling blocks in our movements. Too often, aspects of political practice (for instance, the use of consensus, communal living, rejecting leaders, or following the leadership of those "directly affected") are asserted as articles of faith, or assumed to be transhistorical tenets that anarchists (or members of other political tendencies) have always practiced and therefore always should. When we don't know the origins of such ideas and practices, we have a harder time evaluating how useful they were under previous circumstances and if they are the right tools for the job given conditions today. This leads to a consistent reinvention of political wheels that we frankly don't have time for. For that reason, in this conclusion I draw out lessons, organized into four broad themes, that I believe the history of MNS can teach us about contemporary political struggle.

Opposing, We Propose; Proposing, We Oppose

One of the most significant dilemmas that MNS helps us think through is the relation between the adversarial and exemplary, the destructive and creative, the oppositional and propositional, moments of social struggle. Political scientist and Bring the Ruckus member Joel Olson recently noted,

> Organizing working-class movements, which was so central to anarchist or anarchistic organizations of the late nineteenth and early twentieth centuries, has given way to creating "autonomous zones" like infoshops, art spaces, affinity groups, and collectives, on the one hand, and glorifying large-scale protests, riots, and sabotage, on the other. But in building infoshops and idolizing insurrection, the American anarchist milieu has let the vital work of organizing fall through the middle.[3]

Prominent theoretical statements and the focus of many recent anarchist efforts support Olson's argument. *The Coming Insurrection*, authored by the anonymous Invisible Committee, upholds the French *banlieue* riots of 2005 as a model for radical activity, and in many respects recapitulates the antiorganization strategy of late nineteenth-century insurrectionary anarchists who, with the legendary theorist Mikhail Bakunin, believed "the passion for destruction is at the same time a creative passion."[4] Because they believed that humans' inherently altruistic

and cooperative natures would flower once oppressive institutions were eliminated, classic insurrectionists held that
revolutionary struggle should take an essentially demoli-
tionist approach: prompt a mass insurrection to topple the
existing order, and the rest would follow.

On the other hand, in his recent book *Crack
Capitalism*, John Holloway reverses Bakunin's formulation.
For Holloway, the creative act is also a destructive one. He
urges a focus on creating autonomous zones, noncapital-
ist social relations, and moments of joy, with the belief that
the spreading of such hopeful activities will serve to expand
and connect already-existing "cracks" in the capitalist social order, eventually causing it to shatter.[5] This strategy,
focused overwhelmingly on the creative or prefigurative
moment, shares many similarities with nineteenth-century
utopian socialist currents that sought to create models of a
new social order, in the form of intentional communities,
which they thought would spread by weight of example.[6]

These are not the only voices in the current debate
over strategy and priorities, though. In the wake of a
large-scale inquiry into contemporary forms of resistance
in North America, the Team Colors Collective asserts,
"Movement-building of the kind required now must find
its motor in radical community organizing. Yet how this
is defined, what it looks and feels like, how this functions—these are all moving targets."[7] I believe that the
history of MNS provides a generative perspective on the
creative as well as destructive moments of radical social
transformation—one that doesn't let the crucial work of
organizing fall through the middle, and that also helps

us zero in on a clearer understanding of what constitutes radical community organizing.

The MNS experience points toward the political potential of long-term organizations that actively oppose all forms of social domination through a delicate balance of strategic organizing campaigns and prefigurative activity. In the early 1970s, MNS members developed a theory of revolutionary change that encompassed these and a variety of other elements. Their experiences over the next two decades lent credence to some aspects of this theory, but also highlighted areas where the theory needed to be further developed.

MNS believed that change could and should happen on many different levels—the individual, institutional, community, and system as a whole. As Raasch-Gilman explained (see "Conversations" section above), the group held out hope that a mass movement (or a "movement of movements") would develop that at some point in the future would prevent our current set of unjust institutions from operating by means of a coordinated withdrawal of consent and a mass refusal to participate in their workings. This moment of withdrawal of consent might be seen as a form of general strike or insurrection carried out through nonviolent means. MNS did not posit this moment as the totality or even as the final step of a revolution. Rather, members saw it as one point in a complex process of social transformation in which other components were just as crucial.

MNS believed that for a mass withdrawal of consent to become possible, millions of people needed to adopt radical values and visions as their own, and feel empowered enough to assert them collectively. It also insisted on the need to create well thought-out and time-tested institutions that could fill the "power vacuum" created by the moment of insurrection, if it ever arrived. Members recognized that the spread of these values and this sense of possibility was hard work that required them to participate in adversarial organizing campaigns. Their theory argued that people joined movements, and recognized their individual and collective power, when they won concessions (reforms) from the powerful. Therefore, MNS encouraged members and those they trained to dedicate themselves to the interconnected processes of building prefigurative counterinstitutions, and organizing campaigns to win concessions. They thought that these aspects of struggle should be carried out repeatedly and continuously, building on one another, with the intention of creating sufficient awareness, participation, and power to make more sweeping transformations possible and sustainable in revolutionary moments.

For a decade or more, prefigurative politics has been a central concept and buzzword within the antiauthoritarian Left. Prefiguration is a potentially powerful idea, but it has been applied to such a variety of activities that it can prevent us from clearly distinguishing between different forms of action and the value we believe they hold. The MNS "case study" can help us sort out and assess a variety of claims about prefigurative politics. It can also help us theorize the relationship that prefigurative activity has with other aspects of social change, such as organizing campaigns, direct action, and insurrection.

MNS believed in and practiced different types of prefigurative activity. The first might usefully be termed prefigurative counterinstitutions. These could include self-managed businesses, free health clinics, land trusts that remove housing from the market, neighborhood safety committees, and assemblies or councils that allow the residents of a community to democratically make decisions as a whole. MNS members point to two distinct benefits of such institutions. First, some of them work to promote and support organizing in a variety of ways. Effective counter-institutions (such as food co-ops and mediation centers) have the potential to demonstrate concrete benefits of the work undertaken by the radicals who launch them, helping to legitimize their ideas and beliefs. Such institutions don't typically convert others to a radical perspective out of the sheer weight of their example but they can promote conversation, trust, and collaboration. Additionally, some counterinstitutions (such as collective households) can reduce living expenses and time devoted to wage labor, freeing up time for radicals to commit to organizing campaigns.

A second, and distinct, function of counterinstitutions is to develop participatory, egalitarian, efficient, and trustworthy institutions that can begin to provide services typically fulfilled by states and for-profit enterprises, reducing reliance on them and draining them of their legitimacy. Moreover, they are powerful means of indicating, in the most concrete fashion possible, that, as the saying goes, another world is possible.[8]

To be truly prefigurative, such counterinstitutions would have to undermine, rather than solidify, social hierarchies among the people who staff and use them. MNS believed that these new institutions could step into the breach caused by a mass withdrawal of consent from our current institutions and supply the basis of a new social order. In working to satisfy people's concrete needs outside institutions of domination, such counterinstitutions constitute a form of direct action, which Cindy Milstein usefully describes as "positive direct action" since the activity proactively accomplishes some important task.[9]

As Irwin and other former MNS members emphasized in the "Conversations" section, however, new institutions created by radicals don't always serve these purposes. Irwin helpfully distinguishes between alternative institutions and counterinstitutions. When creative radical projects aren't aimed at movement building, they can end up functioning more like clubhouses for self-selecting radicals, and can appear as irrelevant or off-putting to people whom organizers would like to become more politically active. Such institutions may improve the lives of self-selecting participants in real ways—say, by providing them the opportunity to work less or step outside limiting gender roles. This is crucial and beneficial in itself. But distanced from other aspects of struggle, Irwin is correct that such projects are more accurately labeled alternative rather than counterinstitutions because they don't pose a significant threat to oppressive social relations (and may in fact bolster them). In hindsight, MNS members recognized that another form of prefiguration—prefigurative lifestyle, or what they called living the revolution now—was often reinforced by alternative institutions, and also lead to politically ambiguous outcomes. I return to this below.

As we have seen, MNS sought to balance the development of prefigurative counterinstitutions with adversarial organizing campaigns. They contributed to campaigns against nuclear power plants, the deployment of Cruise missiles, male sexual violence, and many other efforts. If they still existed today, they would likely help the Coalition of Immokalee Workers fight for better conditions for migrant farmworkers and join the efforts to break the siege of Gaza imposed by the state of Israel.[10] MNS recognized the power of direct action tactics such as blockades and building occupations, in which participants did not petition representatives but instead directly hindered violence or injustice from taking place. These are instances of what Milstein refers to as "negative direct action," since the action is taken to oppose or negate some injustice.[11] Yet it is important to note that MNS viewed such negative direct action tactics as elements of larger campaigns focused on organizing groups of people to strategically press their demands against bosses, state officials, and other targets in order to win real, if limited, changes. New opportunities were created through such campaigns to proactively engage with nonradicals, with the intention of trying to move them to take action.

MNS advocated that a third form of prefigurative activity, distinct from building counterinstitutions and practicing prefigurative lifestyles, could and should come into play during organizing campaigns. MNS members sought to develop and inculcate organizational structures as well as norms of interacting that did not replicate the authoritarian, divisive, and demeaning institutions and relationships they were resisting. Like many contemporary antiauthoritarian organizers, members looked to SNCC, one of the most important organizations of the midcentury black freedom movement, as a prime example of this style of organizing. In its first five years, SNCC tried to practice group-centered leadership that empowered participants, rather than encouraging them to simply follow the decisions and orders of one or two charismatic leaders. SNCC members Ella Baker and Bob Moses insisted that if the goal of radical activism is to create situations where all people have the capacity to actively govern themselves and their affairs, movements should not view them simply as bodies put into motion by a small core of organizers but rather as people developing the capacities to define their own goals and shape their own campaigns.[12] Chris Dixon has recently described this as a commitment to practice "non-instrumental organizing" because it insists that people are not just instruments or tools to be used by others.[13] It was in the group's attempts to practice (prefigurative) nonauthoritarian social relationships and noninstrumental organizing that MNS learned critical lessons about consensus and leadership through an extensive trial-and-error process. I will return to these lessons shortly as well.

The MNS experience indicates that while counterinstitutions have the *potential* to bolster organizing campaigns, the opposite is also true: organizing campaigns can serve to bolster counterinstitutions. The contact and discussions with previously inactive people that result from noninstrumental organizing help inform radicals of the types of counterinstitutions (a computer center, a bakery that provides jobs to people coming out of prison, and so on) that people want and need.[14] Being rooted in organizing for change helps keep those focused on institution building from inadvertently constructing insular projects for the radical minority (such as some infoshops, pirate radio stations, and other projects), or alternative institutions that are either ignored or recuperated by the state and capital (such as some domestic violence shelters across the United States and food co-ops in gentrifying neighborhoods).

Running organizing campaigns *in combination* with building counterinstitutions, and with a view toward paralyzing and toppling the system, also works to prevent such campaigns from becoming solely reformist. Reforms pursued without a reconstructive vision remain within the gambit of liberal democratic politics and frequently provide little of the inspiration needed to compel the sacrifices required of committed radicals. Autonomist Marxists and others have also convincingly argued that gains won by oppressed social groups have often, ironically, pushed capitalists, white supremacists, and others with power to respond by developing new technologies and social policies that end up increasing their control while further obscuring relations of domination.[15] To lead to lasting change, reform campaigns need to be chosen for their ability to move increasing numbers of people to struggle by articulating a compelling vision of a better way of living and demonstrating the benefits of taking action.

Drawing on radical pacifist theory, MNS argued that the power of elites ultimately resided in the deference paid to them by ordinary people. They saw that moments of successful revolutionary transition in other countries occurred when the majority of the population collectively ceased to perform the daily activities that allowed the old order to function.[16] Such a situation could not be provoked by attacks on authority figures as old "propaganda of the deed" theorists believed. Rather, it depended on movements that fostered a sense of collective agency and confidence in counterinstitutions. Attempts to promote insurrection without mass support and counterinstitutions prepared to sustain new social relations typically ended in widespread violence, massive repression, and the marginalization of radicals.

In the early 1970s, MNS members thought a moment of mass withdrawal of consent could occur within a decade. As the radical tide of the 1960s ebbed, their hopes that millions of people would soon be ready to take such drastic steps dwindled. Yet the possibility of such a transformative movement remained central to the theory of social change that guided their work, and helped them keep their day-to-day struggles, forms of resistance, and identities as radicals in perspective. At present, this perspective is crucial as a reminder to never stop visioning, aim high, and carry out our work with the big picture in mind, while remaining focused on the immediate tasks that need to happen today, tomorrow, and next month to make those long-range goals possible.

In many respects, the political project outlined by MNS parallels and builds on the strategy and vision of the IWW and anarcho-syndicalists of the early twentieth century. The Wobblies provided one of the most abiding formulations of prefigurative politics when they claimed they were "creating the new world in the shell of the old."[17]

They organized their fellow workers to win concessions from bosses as they built enough support to conduct a general strike, which would overthrow capitalism. The IWW believed that the union itself—the organization created by the workers—would take the place of the old structures following a general strike. For this reason the union needed to operate fairly, and combat bureaucratic and authoritarian tendencies, while still functioning efficiently enough to put the collective boot of tens of thousands of workers to the backsides of the most powerful people the world had ever known.[18] Although it didn't see itself primarily in these terms, MNS was one attempt to envision an expansion of this model beyond the IWW's focus on class struggle to the project of *also* overcoming patriarchy, white supremacy, environmental devastation, and social domination in general.

As this comparison with the Wobblies makes clear, MNS didn't hatch its ideas out of thin air. It instead can be seen as one node in a long-running tradition of political theory and activity that has gone under a variety of names. This becomes even more evident when it is seen that ideas posed by MNS in the 1970s also align closely with the principles of action recently promoted by Michael Hardt and Antonio Negri at the end of their coauthored book *Commonwealth*. Hardt and Negri insist that "we are not faced with an alternative—either insurrection or institutional struggle," but rather that revolution must simultaneously be both. "Revolutions," they claim, "must have democracy as their object and thus the direction and content of revolutionary transition must be defined by the increase of the capacities for democracy of the multitude."[19] Building people's capacities for self-government was at the heart of MNS's vision of how revolution might be accomplished in the late twentieth century. This was one reason that members placed a premium on training others in egalitarian decision-making processes as well as developing counterinstitutions.

When speaking of methods, Hardt and Negri also share much in common with MNS members' evaluation of the benefits of nonviolence. The authors assert, "Revolution does not necessarily require bloodshed, but it does call for the use of force.... In fact, our estimation is that increasingly today a 'disarmed multitude' is much more effective than an armed band and that exodus is more powerful than frontal assault." Moreover, they note that "in evaluating the weapons and forms of violence in revolutionary struggles, the question of effectiveness against the enemy should always be secondary to that of its effects on the multitude and the process of building its institutions."[20] As Lakey contended in the above interview, revolutionary nonviolence is distinct from liberal pacifism because rather than seeking to avoid conflict, nonviolent revolutionaries insist on confrontation by mobilizing a nonviolent, but coercive force of refusal. The secrecy required and dangers associated with violent action (the death or long-term imprisonment of revolutionaries; alienation of those one is fighting with and for) also frequently impede the positive program of building institutions and growing the numbers of active participants, which must be the movement's first priorities.[21] In this sense, another lesson emerges from MNS's reflections on the place of violence within social movements struggling to end domination and violence.

Radical and Anarchist Pacifism

MNS serves as a reminder that radical pacifist philosophy shaped twentieth-century anarchism in fundamental ways. Though MNS as a whole did not identify as anarchist, its relationship to anarchist groups that preceded as well as followed it helps us recognize that the anarchist movement, in the United States and internationally, has historically contained a significant anarchist pacifist strand (alongside insurrectionary, syndicalist, and other tendencies) that merits reconsideration and greater appreciation in the current period. The anarchist pacifist tradition extends, at least, from Leo Tolstoy and Gustav Landauer in the late nineteenth century to Bart de Ligt in the 1930s, influencing Gandhi in the process.[22] During and shortly after World War II, U.S. anarchists such as Dorothy Day and David Dellinger picked up these threads, and passed core concepts on to anarchist and quasi-anarchist groups such as MNS active in the 1970s and 1980s. Participants in the direct action movements of these years, such as Starhawk and David Solnit, in turn relayed anarcho-pacifist ideas and practices to sectors of the global justice movement at the turn of the millennium.[23]

The tradition provides many analytic and tactical insights.[24] As we have seen, it was one of the most important conduits of certain forms of prefigurative politics. Likewise, the radical pacifist insistence on placing violence—and especially "social violence" broadly conceived—as the central object of critique helped facilitate the shift in anarchist theory from a focus on capitalism and the state to a broader, intersectional analysis of social domination in general. This can be glimpsed in the links that former MNS members draw between violence and social hierarchy, nonviolent forms of struggle and antihierarchical organizational forms. As the excerpt from *Why Nonviolence?* included here indicates, radical pacifists have also developed a wealth of knowledge about how to prevail in strategic pressure campaigns by controlling representations of protesters, winning allies, neutralizing fence-sitters, and other means. Today, common opposition to gender, state, and other forms of violence provide a critical basis for links among anarchists, feminists, and prison abolitionists, such as those active in Critical Resistance and INCITE! Women of Color against Violence.[25]

Although there is not enough room here to explore their many implications, the radical and anarchist pacifist traditions seem especially worthy of reconsideration in the current moment. We live in a period in which some European anarchist and other Left groupings have returned to the tactics of mail bombs and physical assaults on political figures. Meanwhile, indisputable proof exists that federal and local authorities in North America have used agent provocateurs to encourage acts of property destruction and violence by radicals as a central component of their policing strategy.[26] Taken together, these developments recall the late nineteenth-century period in which anarchism bogged down in a cycle of infiltration, amoral violence, and paranoia.[27] It was only when respected figures such as Peter Kropotkin and Errico Malatesta eschewed insurrectionary strategies in favor of syndicalism that anarchism regained a modicum of momentum.[28] Fifty years later, during the cold war, radical and anarchist pacifists sought to establish a position of high moral ground by promoting the dignity of all people outside and opposed to both the authoritarian Communist and liberal capitalist camps into which the world was becoming increasingly divided. Today they have the potential to anchor a third pole, this time outside the clash of market and religious fundamentalisms.

Reconsiderations

If MNS's history provides lessons regarding strategy and tactics, it also suggests that it is important to rethink received wisdom on the "organization question." MNS indicates that movements can be severely hindered by a fetishization of the consensus decision-making process along with a rejection of leaders and leadership *tout court*. In recent decades, many antiauthoritarians have seen the use of consensus-based decision-making processes as a barometer of whether an organization or initiative is truly radical or not. As the case of the new SDS in the mid-2000s exemplified, extreme resistance to organizational forms that make it possible for organizers to devise precise political positions, a common strategy, and nationally coordinated actions remains commonplace. Frequently, even democratic organizational structures, if they delineate any roles for members or allow for any decisions to be made by less than the entire membership, are rejected—typically through a hazy conflation of the terms leadership, centralization, and authoritarian. These intense convictions spring from somewhere, but antiauthoritarians who espouse them are often vague on their theoretical or experiential origins.

While concerns around leadership and decision making have been central to Left debates since the nineteenth century, I have argued in this book that MNS was among the most significant organizations promoting contemporary forms of consensus decision making and decentralized organization in the period just prior to our own. MNS saw its use of such techniques as experiments deployed to correct for specific problems (such as patriarchal and egotistic leadership styles) from a political period prior to *its* own and in order to function differently from the institutions it was resisting. Members thought such techniques and organizational forms should be tested, evaluated, and improved upon repeatedly. MNS came to greatly modify and qualify its endorsement of consensus and fully decentralized organizations over time, because it recognized certain ways these practices limited its ability to overcome racism, sexism, capitalism, and imperialism. Nor was it the first organization in the antiauthoritarian tradition to do so.

Sam Dolgoff, an IWW organizer and one of the individuals most responsible for keeping the anarchist tradition alive in the mid-twentieth century, spoke out regularly against the anarchists of his own day who rejected all forms of organization within the movement. During an interview in 1964, Dolgoff offered conclusions similar to those arrived at by MNS, in his own no-nonsense style:

> I think that all organization carries within itself the germ of bureaucratization. I don't really believe that we will ever get rid of it fully. So that reduces the problem to the proposition of reducing the dangers of usurpation of power, or bureaucratization, to its minimum. To say that we need no organization at all is, of course, simply fantastic and idiotic in view of the interdependence of social life and the fact that man is by nature a social being who must combine with his fellow man in order to achieve common aims. So we must have organization, and the problem revolves around, as I said before, the problem of reducing to a minimum the apparent and real danger of concentration of power.[29]

For this reason, it is unfortunate and ironic that many of those who defend their insistence on consensus and extreme decentralization by appealing to this historical tradition, fail to acknowledge the qualifications that also comprise the tradition. Let me thus briefly reiterate points made throughout this book regarding consensus, organization, and leadership.

MNS members state that making decisions by consensus helped their group to develop a common political perspective and build trust with one another when the organization was first forming. As Lakey puts it, consensus was useful when they were "searching" for new ideas. Brigham explains that consensus worked well within small- and medium-size local MNS working groups, but had considerable drawbacks at the regional and national levels.

Raasch-Gilman believes consensus remains the best decision-making process for groups involved in certain types of political work, such as high-risk direct actions, assuming it's practiced with care by people familiar with the process.

Yet Lakey also unequivocally maintains that the "downsides" of consensus contributed to MNS's demise. In his experience, the style of communication and time requirements embedded in the consensus process often prove off-putting or prohibitive to working-class organizers; using it can therefore limit who is involved in an organization or action. Consensus slowed MNS's process of developing new political positions and literature to almost a standstill. Furthermore, Lakey and Irwin argue that consensus hindered MNS's ability to evolve with the times and correct for defects in its strategy, since the requirement that everyone agree to change made staying the same the default position.

Richard Taylor also makes it clear that the MNS founders never intended to imply that their model of consensus should be the way society as a whole should make all decisions—in his view, this was an unrealistic fantasy, ignorant of time constraints and other important aspects of democratic process. MNS members seem to now agree that consensus was a method borrowed from Quaker religious practices and interpersonal counseling models that has some benefits as well as drawbacks when used as a tool within political settings. In their experience, it is most helpful when used to develop new ideas and unity within a self-selecting group, when everyone expected to use it has been trained in the process, in socially homogeneous groups, and when a full commitment is required to undertake risky work.

MNS members also realized that somewhere along the line, their criticisms of old styles of leadership had hardened into a simplistic hostility toward "leaders" and "leadership." They noticed that this short-circuited their work in a variety of ways. First, it prevented many people from giving their all or putting their particular talents to work for the organization from fear of being labeled someone seeking to take charge, show off, and dominate the group. Second, they noticed that despite claims to being leaderless, certain people still ended up bottom-lining projects, making decisions, and serving as go-to people when others needed types of knowledge, contacts with other organizations, and other resources. This pattern of informal or unrecognized leadership was problematic for a couple reasons. It functioned less accountably than if responsibilities and positions had been democratically elected or delegated (with expectations and an evaluation process clearly defined). And those doing the work were often not recognized, frequently leading people to feel underappreciated and burnt-out.

In response to this situation, MNS deconstructed the term leader, which had become overburdened with associations. In the pamphlet *Leadership for Change* and other publications, MNS members argued that leadership was really just the process of practicing a number of different important skills and qualities, such as follow-through, providing inspiration, knowledge derived from having completed a given task numerous times, mediating disagreements, creative problem solving, and communicating effectively. Surely it was counterproductive for a group to expect one or two members to embody all these qualities, just as it was counterproductive for one or two members to, in effect, hog all these qualities by not helping others to develop them. MNS highlights that leadership qualities are resources that should be shared and nurtured. We all have the capacity to exercise some of them, and to the greatest extent possible, we should.

As MNS members refined their ideas about leadership, they also began to acknowledge that some delegation of responsibility for coordinating and developing their organization was needed, and was preferable to organizational stagnation, or allowing it to happen spontaneously and haphazardly. This meant accepting some degree of both centralization and hierarchy—words that unsettled them as much as they do most anarchists today. Yet they did it anyway, and they seem to agree that it was the right decision. All the MNS members I've spoken with continue to reject Leninist/democratic centralist organizational models as well as the meritocratic and careerist forms often found in liberal nonprofits and advocacy groups. But their experience also showed them the pitfalls of what they called spontaneous models of organizing and encouraged them to develop, through trial and error, an empowerment model instead.

They admit that this is an unfinished task, but their efforts provide us with helpful starting points. It is useful, for example, to distinguish between *organizational* and *social hierarchies*, and between *delegated* and *coercive authority*. That is, our organizations should seek to avoid reproducing hierarchies between social groups (such as men and women, or white people and people of color).

Yet we can acknowledge that divisions of labor can be useful and are often necessary if we are focused on winning specific campaigns. The jobs of coordinating the work along with developing the skills and capacities of others are not automatically oppressive (though they frequently are done in oppressive ways). In fact, such roles can promote empowerment by helping others to develop their capacities or achieve a goal that can only be reached through collaboration.

Rather than reject organizational structures and delegated leadership roles out of hand, MNS, like many movements highly respected by North American antiauthoritarians (for instance, the Zapatistas and the Aymara people engaged in resource wars in Bolivia), ended up inventing forms that worked to maximize leadership development, self-management, and the rotation of administrative positions while still accomplishing other necessary tasks. Theorists and radicals from Latin America, such as Raúl Zibechi and Enrique Dussel, have devoted considerable work to defining these styles of organization in recent years, putting special attention on the principle of *mandar obedeciendo*: leading or governing by obeying. Likewise, Michael Albert and Robin Hahnel have argued that social movement organizations and counterinstitutions should create "balanced job complexes," as described in their participatory economics model, as one means of refusing to reinforce social hierarchies.[30] Organizational experiments should continue, but they will be much more productive if they start from these and other principles derived from concrete instances of radical struggle, rather than from the hypothesis that all forms of organization and leadership hinder the work of radical social transformation.

Prefiguring Racial Justice

As we have seen, MNS members forthrightly acknowledge that one of the greatest challenges they faced was becoming a multiracial organization after beginning as one whose members were predominantly white. Today, organizations and social milieus that desire social justice remain more racially and class divided than many of us wish they were. MNS's history provides some lessons, especially for white radicals, in this regard as well.

MNS's inability to become a multiracial organization, after years of concerted effort, was one of the major reasons that members decided to disband in 1988. This decision prompts a consideration of a number of important issues. Most obviously, it implies that building multiracial political movements is important and should be a goal for white organizers. (This is also true of multiclass movements for middle-class organizers, but since MNS was more successful at that, it has been less of a focus in this book.) Why is this the case? It is not that people of color, or working-class people, are automatically more radical or born with a perfect knowledge of what to do, strategically, in a given moment. Nevertheless, history shows that whenever people with some kind of privilege seek to change things for the better, supposedly for everyone, without the active involvement of those with less privilege, the latter's conditions and concerns are nearly always neglected—and often even made worse. Social movements of marginalized peoples have put forward the slogan "Never about us, without us," in response to missionaries, rich philanthropists, and others promising "uplift" without listening to and working with the very people they are claiming to lift up. Likewise, it is regressive for radicals with racial, class, or gender privilege to assume that they could or should make the changes needed today without the active participation and leadership of members of the social groups whose conditions—at least partially—inspire their rage in the first place.

We might also relate this question back to the concern with prefigurative politics. If our ends should be consonant with our means, and we want a nonracist society, we should build a non- and antiracist movement. I've found it curious that anarchists have insisted on using a particular, nuanced consensus process to organize mass actions, claiming that their ideology and vision are articulated in the very methods they use, while they have not been nearly as concerned about what their overwhelmingly white group was prefiguring and proclaiming to the world.[31]

As much as I believe in what I have just written, I also recognize that this line of argument has, in the past decade, sometimes stymied our movements rather than enhanced them, and that is the last thing I want this book to do. It would be a mistake to interpret Lakey and Raasch-Gilman as suggesting that it is better not to act or have no organization at all than to act in predominantly white political formations. The current moment is one in which we need as many radical (and progressive) political organizations, efforts, and organizers as we can get. MNS members hoped their organization could be a major force promoting fundamental social transformation across many aspects of society. They decided, I think quite rightly, that this could not be accomplished by an overwhelmingly white organization.

Most political projects today will have more modest goals, though. There is much that can be accomplished by white or mainly white political groups, *assuming* they recognize antiracism as a principle, and work to develop antiracist consciousness, analysis, and multiracial alliances. This is especially true when such groups are operating in primarily white communities or challenging white racism.[32] The former MNS members also emphasized the fact that they dissolved MNS so that they would be able to devote their energy to new projects that they believed might be able to accomplish more—*not* to become inactive, or paralyzed by their own shortcomings, guilt, or fears of being criticized. The point is to work toward building organizations and movements with ideal racial, class, and other dynamics. Counterintuitive as it seems, this sometimes requires working in groups where these dynamics are less than ideal.

The MNS experience suggests that the more white radicals focus on prefigurative lifestyles and counterinstitutions *without organizing*, the more likely it is that they will remain in predominantly white, rather than multiracial, political formations. Members came to recognize that some of their countercultural behaviors and symbols made them appear to be an insular clique that many people of other racial (as well as class and age) backgrounds felt uncomfortable participating in. One former member, Betsy Leondar-Wright, recalls a time when MNS members were participating in a community-organizing project meeting held at the house of an older woman not affiliated with MNS. During a break, Leondar-Wright used the bathroom and intentionally refrained from flushing the toilet after urinating, as was common practice (for environmental reasons) in the Philadelphia MNS houses. Flushing would waste water, violating her values, her commitment to live as she would after the revolution. On the other hand, she was in someone else's house, and not flushing might offend this woman's own values, putting strain on MNS's ability to work with her and the community organization. One of Leondar-Wright's comrades used the bathroom after her and flushed for them both. In retrospect she was glad that he did.[33]

I've seen similar tensions arise countless times while doing political work more recently. My own exposure to radical politics first came through my involvement with the punk scene. That counterculture places a lot of emphasis on practicing prefigurative lifestyles, and making political statements through consumer decisions and bodily display. When punks have only served food from dumpsters or refused to have options for meat eaters, when they have shunned deodorant or insisted on playing music (even with the most radical lyrics) that sounded like abrasive noise to others, they have at times inadvertently created barriers to movement building when they were *trying* to demonstrate a better way of living.[34] The shared sense of acting and being different from the bulk of the world when one is working with other radicals can be one of the most thrilling and rewarding things about being an activist. Sometimes it feels like the only thing that keeps us going.

But what we need to realize is that people who want to change the world come from many places, have different visions of what that new world will be like, do their political work in different ways, and feel glimmers of those new worlds in a whole variety of rebel cultures. Our rebel countercultures are nearly always linked to our structural positions (such as our genders, races, classes, and nationalities), and those distinctions are usually much easier for people in other structural positions to see than the fact that we are participating in a resistant counterculture. To keep things in perspective, I've found that it is often useful to ask, "When I think I'm acting like an anarchist, are people perceiving me to be acting like, say, a white and/or middleclass and/or male and/or straight person? Am I? Is this going to be a problem?"

It is also important to note that these challenges arise most frequently for radicals dedicated to a multifaceted politics that recognize numerous vectors of domination that can cut across one another. In the question-and-answer section earlier, Lakey described one such dilemma: Would being openly gay in the neighborhood hamper MNS's efforts to organize against white flight? In this example, the members decided it was worth the risk—queer liberation was as central to their politics as fighting racist real estate practices. Sorting through decisions such as these, Leondar-Wright articulated the concepts of "essential" and "inessential weirdness." In her work helping organizers build cross-class alliances, she explains that one of the most common mistakes middle-class organizers make is "imposing inessential weirdness" on mixed-class groups. She has even created a rubric to help others evaluate when their weirdness is essential or not![35] This goes to show that there is not a simple standard for all times and places, such as "expression or prefiguration should always be squashed to facilitate organizing." Rather, there are multiple factors at play, such as whether or not you are in someone else's house—literally or figuratively speaking.

Most important, the stories that Nina Huizinga and others shared when they described MNS's work indicate that it *is* possible to overcome these initial impressions and divisions. They are not absolute by any means; however, they frequently take specific efforts to transcend. MNS members found it easiest to bridge race and class divides when participating in organizing campaigns in which they fought to achieve common goals with people outside their organization as well as from different social backgrounds. Sometimes MNS initiated these efforts, like in the neighborhood safety/antipolice campaign. At other times, such as the walk-in homesteading campaign, they took the lead from political organizations formed by people of color. Instead of trying to tell these groups how to conduct their meetings or why they should make more radical demands, MNS members carried out work that was requested of them.

Today, organizations such as the Catalyst Project, which help white activists develop antiracist consciousness and organizing skills, encourage those who feel trapped in the "student activist ghetto" or "punk ghetto" (in the same way that some MNS members felt trapped in the "peace ghetto") to engage in this sort of solidarity and support work whenever it is feasible. The point, again, is not that radicals with some form of privilege should always take directions or await requests for help from those on the other side of that hierarchy. Rather, those committed to change need to be humble and learn about the ways that other people are struggling, to do what it takes to build the personal bonds on which strong social movements arise.

Finding or becoming individuals who can bridge the divides created by social hierarchies is crucial to the process of organizing powerful movements. This is another place where movement experience, personal relationships, reputation, and trust—all aspects of leadership—become essential. Such "bridge leaders" frequently have their feet planted in two or more social groups simultaneously, or have a variety of experiences under their belts that give them big-picture perspective as well as insights about the norms, assumptions, and ways of getting work done common to people of different classes, races, occupations, and movement sectors. Overcoming class, race, religious, gender, and other divisions to build diverse and representative movements are some of the hardest challenges that organizers face—precisely because these are the divisions that maintain our unjust social system.

Carrying on the Work

In the introduction, I referred to this book as an experiment in militant and coresearch. Those terms derive originally from the practice of radical Italian intellectuals studying the working conditions, opinions, and forms of resistance of everyday working people in the 1950s and 1960s.[36] Their research was primarily ethnographic, whereas this project has been more historical. There are significant parallels, however. For one, both research projects were carried out with the intention of directly informing and heightening contemporary political movements. Second, both sought to bring out the wisdom and voices of underappreciated social change agents, as opposed to asserting the overriding importance of intellectuals and their abstract theorems for achieving revolution.

One of the key benefits of doing this kind of militant coresearch, I've discovered, is that it often prompts wider forms of intergenerational dialogue and movement building. I have tried to organize this book in a way that exposes some of that process and prompts you to extend it. My historical research is presented here next to the voices of the people who made that history as well as a few documents that became archival long before they should have been. The questions raised by other radicals and constructive feedback offered by former MNS members prompted me, in this conclusion, to refine and elaborate on lessons only alluded to in the original article, which now forms the "History" section of this book. Rather than being anywhere near comprehensive, the ideas presented here reflect some of the significant lessons suggested by MNS members, my analysis of their history, and my own experiences in recent years.

Along the way, I have been inspired by the brilliance, commitment, and generosity of the former MNS members with whom I collaborated on this project, to say nothing of the organizing work they continue to take on into their sixties and seventies. I hope you feel the same way, and will communicate with them and me if you are interested in carrying on the conversations that comprise this book. I'm perhaps most impressed with how seriously MNS members took themselves and the scope of their ambitions.

At the conclusion of his remarks, Lakey stated, "I have this confidence welling up in me now that when you organize your equivalent of MNS, it will be better than ours." I'm eager to draw on the inspiration and crucial lessons that MNS offers, and in collaboration with many others, prove him right.

Notes

Introduction

1. See http://www.naasn.org.

Movement for a New Society and Contemporary Anarchism

1. On the international and libertarian aspects of the movements of 1968, see George Katsiaficas, *The Imagination of the New Left: A Global Analysis of 1968* (Boston: South End Press, 1987).

2. Throughout this book, I refer to the organization as MNS rather than *the* MNS in accordance with the preferences of its former members. Since their efforts never reached the scale of a mass social movement, these members feel it is more accurate and modest to emphasize that "MNS" is a proper noun, the name of the organization, rather than a historical phenomenon, as "the Movement for a New Society" might imply.

3. The sociologist Wini Breines coined the term prefigurative politics to describe a central feature of the approach taken by

the Students for a Democratic Society: the attempt to "create and sustain within the lived practice of the movement, relationships and political forms that 'prefigured' and embodied the desired society." Wini Breines, *Community and Organization in the New Left, 1962–1968: The Great Refusal*, 2nd ed. (New Brunswick, NJ: Rutgers University Press, 1989), 6. See also Francesca Polletta, *Freedom Is an Endless Meeting: Democracy in American Social Movements* (Chicago: University of Chicago, 2002), 6–12; Cindy Milstein, *Anarchism and Its Aspirations* (Oakland, CA: Institute for Anarchist Studies and AK Press, 2010), 68–70.

4. Throughout this chapter, I refer to "alternative institutions" created by MNS. In the next chapter, former MNS member Robert Irwin argues that "counterinstitutions" is a preferable term. I agree with him, and further distinguish between the two in the conclusion. I have left the term "alternative institutions" intact in this chapter so as not to confuse the reader and to make transparent the dialogic nature of this research project.

5. See Scott H. Bennett, *Radical Pacifism: The War Resisters League and Gandhian Nonviolence in America, 1915–1963* (Syracuse: Syracuse University Press, 2003); Marian Mollin, *Radical Pacifism in Modern America: Egalitarianism and Protest* (Philadelphia: University of Pennsylvania Press, 2006); James Tracy, *Direct Action: Radical Pacifism from the Union Eight to the Chicago Seven* (Chicago: University of Chicago Press, 1996).

6. Bart de Ligt, *The Conquest of Violence: An Essay on War and Revolution* (1937; repr., London: Pluto Press, 1989).

7. See Alan Antliff, *Anarchy and Art: From the Paris Commune to the Fall of the Berlin Wall* (Vancouver: Arsenal Pulp Press, 2007); Dachine Rainer, "Holley Cantine: February 14, 1916–January 2, 1977," *Drunken Boat: Art, Rebellion, Anarchy* 2

(1994): 177–85; Taylor Stoehr, Preface to *Drawing the Line Once Again: Paul Goodman's Anarchist Writings*, ed. Taylor Stoehr, 5–18 (Oakland, CA: PM Press, 2010).

8. I examine these developments in detail in "A New Anarchism Emerges, 1940–1954," *Journal for the Study of Radicalism* 5, no. 1 (Spring 2011): 105–32.

9. Polletta, *Freedom Is an Endless Meeting*, 26–54.

10. See Maurice Isserman, *If I Had a Hammer: The Death of the Old Left and the Birth of the New Left* (Urbana: University of Illinois Press, 1987); Van Gosse, *Rethinking the New Left: An Interpretive History* (New York: Palgrave Macmillan, 2005).

11. See Max Elbaum, *Revolution in the Air: Sixties Radicals Turn to Lenin, Mao, and Che* (New York: Verso, 2002); Dan Berger, *Outlaws of America: The Weather Underground and the Politics of Solidarity* (Oakland, CA: AK Press, 2005).

12. See Polletta, *Freedom Is an Endless Meeting*, 149–75; Sara Evans, *Personal Politics: The Roots of Women's Liberation in the Civil Rights Movement and the New Left* (New York: Vintage, 1979); Alice Echols, *Daring to Be Bad: Radical Feminism in America, 1967–1975* (Minneapolis: University of Minnesota Press, 1989).

13. George Lakey, personal communication with author, July 9, 2008.

14. See George Lakey, *Strategy for a Living Revolution* (San Francisco: W. H. Freeman and Company, 1973), xiii–xviii.

15. "Program for a New Society: A Statement by A Quaker Action Group," leaflet, Wisconsin Historical Society, Social Action vertical file, box 1, A Quaker Action Group folder.

16. Lynne Shivers, "Short-term Trainer's Collective at the Life Center," *Dandelion*, December 1971, n.p.; *Dandelion*, December

1973, n.p.; "Movement Building—National," *Dandelion*, October 1972, n.p.; Betsy Raasch-Gilman, "The Movement for a New Society: One Participant's Account," unpublished memoir, 17, Swarthmore College Peace Collection, Movement for a New Society Collection, DG 154, acc. 02A-025, box 6.

17. Berit Lakey and Paul Morrisey, "Hello . . . Goodbye, I Say Hello," *Dandelion*, June 1973, n.p.

18. Susanne Gowan, George Lakey, William Moyer, and Richard Taylor, *Moving toward a New Society* (Philadelphia: New Society Press, 1976); George Lakey, *Strategy for a Living Revolution*.

19. "Finding Out," *Dandelion*, October 1973, n.p.

20. Intersectionality is a concept developed by feminist women of color to theorize the experience of having one's life shaped by multiple forms of oppression that operate simultaneously, and coconstitute and reinforce one another. See Kimberlé Crenshaw Williams, "Mapping the Margins: Intersectionality, Identity Politics, and Violence against Women of Color," in *The Public Nature of Private Violence*, ed. Martha Albertson Fineman and Rixanne Mykitiuk, 93–118 (New York: Routledge, 1994); Combahee River Collective, "A Black Feminist Statement," in *This Bridge Called My Back: Writings by Radical Women of Color*, ed. Gloria Anzaldua and Cherrie Moraga, 210–18 (Boston: Kitchen Table Press, 1982).

21. See, for example, Gowan, Lakey, Moyer, and Taylor, *Moving toward a New Society*, 21–62.

22. "Analysis," *MNS Packet*, Wisconsin Historical Society, Movement for a New Society Records, 1974–77, box 1.

23. On participatory economics, see Michael Albert and Robin Hahnel, *Looking Forward: Participatory Economics for the*

Twenty-First Century (Boston: South End Press, 1991). An earlier work by Albert and Hahnel, *Unorthodox Marxism: An Essay on Capitalism, Socialism, and Revolution* (Boston: South End Press, 1978), was used regularly in the vision section of macroanalysis seminars after it was released.

24. "Vision," *MNS Packet*, Wisconsin Historical Society, Movement for a New Society Records, 1974–77, box 1.

25. "Macro-Analysis Reading List, Revision 9/76" and "Organizing Macro-Analysis Seminars: Study and Action for a New Society, Updated Reading List" (1981), Swarthmore College Peace Collection, MNS Collection, acc. 90A-55, box 6; Murray Bookchin, *Post-Scarcity Anarchism* (Montreal: Black Rose Books, 1971); Dimitri Roussopoulos and C. George Benello, eds., *The Case for Participatory Democracy: Some Prospects for a Radical Society* (Montreal: Black Rose Books, 1972); Sam Dolgoff, *The Anarchist Collectives: Worker's Self-management in Spain, 1936–1939* (New York: Free Life Editions, 1974).

26. Bob Irwin, "On the Organization Question," February 17, 1976, photocopied manuscript, Swarthmore College Peace Collection, MNS Collection, acc. 90A-55, box 9.

27. See Lakey, *Strategy for a Living Revolution*, 67–72; Gowan, Lakey, Moyer, and Taylor, *Moving toward a New Society*, 263–68.

28. "Structure," *MNS Packet*, Wisconsin Historical Society, Movement for a New Society Records, 1974–77, box 1.

29. George Lakey, interview by author and Andrew Willis Garcés, tape recording, Philadelphia, June 28, 2008.

30. Ibid.

31. "Training for Nonviolent Social Change," *MNS Packet*, Wisconsin Historical Society, Movement for a New Society Records, 1974–77, box 1.

32. Lakey, interview.

33. See Lakey, *Strategy for a Living Revolution*, 1–28; Gowan, Lakey, Moyer, and Taylor *Moving toward a New Society*, 217–36.

34. This metaphor is quite similar to Kropotkin's belief that anarchists would serve as "the midwife to the revolution." Both assume a facilitatory rather than an instigative role.

35. Gowan, Lakey, Moyer, and Taylor, *Moving toward a New Society*, 270–81. MNS's conception of revolutionary reforms drew on André Gorz, *Strategy for Labor* (Boston: Beacon Press, 1967).

36. Richard K. Taylor, *Blockade! A Guide to Nonviolent Intervention* (Maryknoll, NY: Orbis, 1977); Richard Taylor, "Blockading for Bangladesh," *Progressive*, February 1972, 20–23. The Associated Press coverage of the blockade was picked up by newspapers across the country. See, for example, "Flotilla of Canoes Fails to Bar Ship," *Corpus Christi Times* (Corpus Christi, TX), July 15, 1971, 50; "Union to Load Non-Military Cargo on Ship to Pakistan," *Cumberland News* (Cumberland, MD), July 17, 1971, 3.

37. Taylor, "Blockading for Bangladesh"; "East Pakistani Freighter 'Barred' at Philadelphia," *Cumberland News*, August 13, 1971, 3.

38. Chuck Fager, "22 Canoes vs. Navy," pamphlet, Wisconsin Historical Society, Social Action vertical file, box 29, folder: Movement for a New Society; "7 Sailors Jump Ship in N.J.," *Bucks County Courier Times* (Bucks County, PA), April 24, 1972, 26; "Seven Sailors Leap Overboard in a Protest," *Bridgeport Telegram* (Bridgeport, CT), April 25, 1972, 31.

39. The fact that neither the Pakistani nor the Vietnam actions developed into longer-standing or extraregional campaigns may provide an early example of the limits of the

movement-building techniques that MNS promoted in the early 1970s.

40. Jim Schrag, "MNS at Wounded Knee: The Network Works," *Dandelion*, June 1973, 1.

41. MNS fund-raising appeal, Spring 1979, Labadie Collection, University of Michigan, vertical file, folder: Socialism—Movement for a New Society.

42. "MNS Structure," *MNS Packet*, Wisconsin Historical Society, Movement for a New Society Records, 1974–77, box 1.

43. "Program for a New Society," in Lakey, *Strategy for a Living Revolution*, 72–78.

44. "Program for a New Society: A Statement by A Quaker Action Group," leaflet, Wisconsin Historical Society, Social Action vertical file, box 1, A Quaker Action Group folder.

45. MNS membership numbers are difficult to calculate, since membership was loosely defined in the organization's first decade. Often small groups that expressed interest in MNS's political vision were considered "part of the network" in internal publications, only to disappear from the record soon afterward. This characterization of the life of MNS members is primarily derived from Raasch-Gilman, "The Movement for a New Society." See also George Lakey, "Catching Up and Moving On: What Can We Learn for the Future from the Movement for a New Society?" manuscript, Swarthmore College Peace Collection, MNS Collection, acc. 90A-55, box 9.

46. Jim Schrag, "Collectives of the Movement for a New Society and 'Friends of MNS' in West Philadelphia," Swarthmore College Peace Collection, MNS Collection, acc. 90A-55, box 15.

47. "The Philadelphia Life Center," *Dandelion*, Spring 1976, n.p.

48. "Neighborhood Block Group Fights Crime, Fear of It," *Dandelion*, October 1973, n.p.

49. "Alternative Institutions," *MNS Packet*, Wisconsin Historical Society, Movement for a New Society Records, 1974–77, box 1; Lakey, interview.

50. Dion Lerman and Scott Burgwin, "Men's Liberation," *Dandelion*, Fall 1975, 9.

51. Raasch-Gilman, "The Movement for a New Society," 64–74; Scott Burgwin, "Re-evaluation Counseling as a Tool for Social Change," *Dandelion*, Spring 1976, 1–3. For a critical analysis of reevaluation counseling, see Mathew Lyons, "Sex, Lies, and Co-counseling," *Activist Men's Journal*, August 1993, available at http://home.comcast.net/~reevaluation-counseling/sexlies.htm.

52. Bill Moyer, "MNS Historical Development Goal to Start the 1980's: Move from the 'Spontaneous' to the 'Empowerment' Organizational Model," January 31, 1981, Swarthmore College Peace Collection, MNS Collection, DG 154, acc. 90A-55, box 10.

53. On former radicals turning to gurus and mysticism, see Christopher Lasch, *The Culture of Narcissism: American Life in an Age of Diminishing Expectations* (New York: W. W. Norton and Company, 1979); Jerry Rubin, *Growing Up at Thirty Seven*, (New York: M. Evans, 1976).

54. "MNS Support Communities," *Dandelion*, Winter 1974, n.p.

55. "Training," *MNS Packet*, Wisconsin Historical Society, Movement for a New Society Records, 1974–77, box 1; Raasch-Gilman, "The Movement for a New Society," 4–15.

56. I thank Chris Dixon for this insight.

57. The spokescouncil, also known as the "small-to-large

group decision-making process," is a form of organization in which representatives of affinity groups meet to communicate their group's ideas and deliberate on issues affecting the larger group, typically using consensus process.

58. Lakey, interview.

59. "MNS at Seabrook," *Dandelion*, Spring 1977, 12–17. For an account of the antinuclear movement, see Barbara Epstein, *Political Protest and Cultural Revolution: Nonviolent Direct Action in the 1970s and 1980s* (Berkeley: University of California Press, 1991).

60. MNS was certainly not the first organization to transform incarceration into an opportunity for movement building. For the free speech fights of the Industrial Workers of the World, see Melvyn Dubofsky, *We Shall Be All: A History of the Industrial Workers of the World* (New York: Quadrangle, 1969), 173–97. For a discussion of "the black public sphere of incarceration" during the civil rights movement, see Houston Baker, "Critical Memory and the Black Public Sphere," in *The Black Public Sphere: A Public Culture Book*, ed. Black Public Sphere Collective, 5–38 (Chicago: University of Chicago Press, 1995).

61. George Lakey, "The Life and Death of the Movement for a New Society," *Friends Journal*, September 1989, 22.

62. Raasch-Gilman, "The Movement for a New Society," 31.

63. On the relation of the utopian socialist tradition to anarchism, see Richard Day, *Gramsci Is Dead: Anarchist Currents in the Newest Social Movements* (London: Pluto Press, 2005), 91–128; Eunice Minette Schuster, *Native American Anarchism* (1932; repr., Port Townsend, WA: Breakout Productions, 1999).

64. Lakey, interview.

65. Gordan Burnside, "A New Manifesto," review of *Moving toward a New Society*, by Susanne Gowan, George Lakey, William Moyer, and Richard Taylor, *Progressive*, August 1976.

66. Richard Taylor, interview by Margaret Allen and Joan Gibson, n.d., Swarthmore College Peace Collection, MNS Collection, acc. 90A-55, box 9.

67. Raasch-Gilman, "The Movement for a New Society," 55.

68. Janet Hilliker, "M.N.S. questions," September 1976, Wisconsin Historical Society, Movement for a New Society Records, 1974–77, box 1.

69. Lakey, interview.

70. Epstein, *Political Protest and Cultural Revolution*, 60.

71. Hyde Park Chapter of the Chicago Women's Liberation Union, "Socialist Feminism: A Strategy for the Women's Movement," quoted in Echols, *Daring to Be Bad*, 6.

72. Bookchin, *Post-Scarcity Anarchism*, 177, 190. For his reevaluation, see Murray Bookchin, *Social Anarchism or Lifestyle Anarchism: An Unbridgeable Chasm* (Oakland, CA: AK Press, 1995).

73. Thomas Frank, *The Conquest of Cool: Business Culture, Counterculture, and the Rise of Hip Consumerism* (Chicago: University of Chicago Press, 1997); *Naomi Klein, No Logo: Taking on the Brand Bullies* (New York: Picador, 1999).

74. George Lakey, "Eleven Years Old: A Perspective on Movement for a New Society in Philadelphia," October 6, 1982, 7, Swarthmore College Peace Collection, MNS Collection, acc. 90A-55, box 10.

75. Ibid., 14.

76. Ibid.; Raasch-Gilman, 22–26, 55.

77. Lakey, "Movement for a New Society: A Case Study of

Network Formation," unpublished typescript in author's possession, 6.

78. Dion Lerman to Janet Hilliker, letter, January 22, 1977, Wisconsin Historical Society, Movement for a New Society Records, 1974–77, box 1.

79. Pamela Haines, "MNS and Strategy," *Dandelion*, Summer–Fall 1977, 7.

80. Bruce Kokopeli and George Lakey, *Leadership for Change: Toward a Feminist Model* (Philadelphia: New Society Publishers, n.d.).

81. Lakey, interview; "Pandora Paper," Swarthmore College Peace Collection, MNS Collection, acc. 90A-55, box 10.

82. Lakey, interview.

83. Lakey, "Catching Up and Moving On," 19.

84. Taylor, interview.

85. Raasch-Gilman, "The Movement for a New Society," 102.

86. Ibid., 108–9.

87. Alan Tuttle to Janet Hilliker, letter January 4 [1977], Wisconsin Historical Society, Movement for a New Society Records, 1974–77, box 1.

88. Hilliker, "M.N.S. questions."

89. Raasch-Gilman, "The Movement for a New Society," 32.

90. Bill Moyer, "MNS Historical Development Goal to Start the 1980's: Move from the 'Spontaneous' to the 'Empowerment' Organizational Model," January 31, 1981, Swarthmore College Peace Collection, MNS Collection, acc. 90A-55, box 10. See also Raasch-Gilman, "The Movement for a New Society," 113.

91. Michael Siptroth, "Directions," *Dandelion Wine*, July 1982, 20–21; Raasch-Gilman, "The Movement for a New Society," 103.

92. Raach-Gilman, "The Movement for a New Society," 103–5, 116.

93. See the July–August 1986 and September 1986 issues of *Grapevine*.

94. Steve Chase, "Some Thoughts after Taking My Foot out of My Mouth," *Grapevine*, July–August 1986, 53.

95. Nancy Brigham, "MNSers as Movement Builders," *Grapevine*, July–August 1986, 42.

96. Raasch-Gilman, "The Movement for a New Society," 133. See also the discussion of "Diversity and MNS" in the May 1986 issue of the *Grapevine*.

97. See the September 1988 issue of the Grapevine; Grace C. Ross, "Ending, Going On: Movement for a New Society," *Peacework*, October 1988, 11.

98. Lakey, *Strategy for a Living Revolution*, 28.

99. See, respectively, http://www.newsociety.com and http://www.mountainmeadow.org.

100. The building that now houses the A-Space, Philadelphia's long-running anarchist community center, and Philadelphia Books through Bars, served as the MNS office throughout much of the organization's existence, and continues to be owned by the land trust started by MNS.

101. Joshua Kahn Russell and Brian Kelly, "Giving Form to a Stampede: The First Two Years of the New Students for a Democratic Society," *Upping the Anti* 6 (May 2008): 84–89.

102. Day, *Gramsci Is Dead*, 18.

103. Ibid., 204–5.

104. "From Our Mailbag," *Vanguard* 2, no. 3 (January–February 1936): 23.

Q&A with Former MNS Members

1. See Bill Moyer, JoAnn McAllister, Mary Lou Finley, and Steven Soifer, *Doing Democracy: The MAP Model for Organizing Social Movements* (Gabriola Island, BC: New Society Publishers, 2001).

MNS and the Current Moment

1. For an insightful examination of previous right-wing populist movements, see Chip Berlet and Mathew N. Lyons, *Right-wing Populism in America: Too Close for Comfort* (New York: Guilford Press, 2000).

2. See, for example, Costas Douzinas and Slavoj Žižek, eds., *The Idea of Communism* (New York: Verso, 2010); Raúl Zibechi, *Dispersing Power: Social Movements as Anti-State Forces*, trans. Ramor Ryan (Oakland, CA: AK Press, 2010); Enrique Dussel, *Twenty Theses on Politics*, trans. George Ciccariello-Maher (Durham, NC: Duke University Press, 2008).

3. Joel Olson, "The Problem with Infoshops and Insurrections: U.S. Anarchism, Movement Building, and the Racial Order," in *Contemporary Anarchist Studies: An Introductory Anthology of Anarchism in the Academy*, ed. Randall Amster, Abraham DeLeon, Luis Fernandez, Anthony J. Nocella II, and Deric Shannon, 35–45 (New York: Routledge, 2009), 36.

4. Bakunin quoted in Mark Leier, *Bakunin: The Creative Passion* (New York: Thomas Dunne, 2006), 98. Invisible Committee, *The Coming Insurrection* (Los Angeles: Semiotext(e), 2009). For the precepts of nineteenth- and early twentieth-century insurrectionary anarchism, see Michael Schmidt and

Lucien van der Walt, *Black Flame: The Revolutionary Class Politics of Anarchism and Syndicalism* (Oakland, CA: AK Press, 2009). For the classical anarchists' understanding of human nature, see George Crowder, *Classical Anarchism: The Political thought of Godwin, Proudhon, Bakunin, and Kropotkin* (Oxford: Oxford University Press, 1992). In recent decades, anarchists influenced by poststructuralist political philosophy have deeply criticized the theories of human subjectivity and power that undergird insurrectionary anarchist strategy. See Todd May, "Anarchism from Foucault to Rancière," in *Contemporary Anarchist Studies: An Introductory Anthology of Anarchism in the Academy*, ed. Randall Amster, Abraham DeLeon, Luis Fernandez, Anthony J. Nocella II, and Deric Shannon, 11–17 (New York: Routledge, 2009); Todd May, *The Political Philosophy of Poststructuralist Anarchism* (University Park: Penn State University Press, 1994); Saul Newman, *The Politics of Postanarchism* (Edinburgh: University of Edinburgh Press, 2010).

5. John Holloway, *Crack Capitalism* (London: Pluto Press, 2010).

6. Richard Day calls for a strategy similar to that proposed by Holloway and explicitly links it to the utopian socialist project in *Gramsci Is Dead: Anarchist Currents in the Newest Social Movements* (London: Pluto Press, 2005).

7. Team Colors Collective, *Wind(s) from Below: Radical Community Organizing to Make a Revolution Possible* (Portland, OR: Team Colors, 2010), 94. See also Team Colors Collective, *Uses of a Whirlwind: Movement, Movements, and Contemporary Radical Currents in the United States* (Oakland, CA: AK Press, 2010).

8. While I am skeptical that the creation of counterinstitutions should be the singular priority of anticapitalist struggle,

Holloway's impassioned argument for their importance to the process of transformation in *Crack Capitalism* is, to my mind, convincing and quite moving. For another voice calling on us to cease viewing capital as omnipresent and impenetrable, see J. K. Gibson-Graham, *The End of Capitalism (As We Knew It): A Feminist Critique of Political Economy* (Minneapolis: University of Minnesota Press, 2006).

9. Cindy Milstein, *Anarchism and Its Aspirations* (Oakland, CA: AK Press, 2010), 70.

10. For the Coalition of Immokalee Workers, see http://www.ciw-online.org. On international efforts to achieve a free Palestine, see http://www.bdsmovement.net and http://www.endtheoccupation.org. Reports and analysis on both of these efforts are available at http://www.leftturn.org.

11. Milstein, *Anarchism and Its Aspirations*, 70.

12. See Charles Payne, *I've Got the Light of Freedom: The Organizing Tradition and the Mississippi Freedom Struggle*, 2nd ed. (Berkeley: University of California Press, 2007); Barbara Ransby, *Ella Baker and the Black Freedom Movement: A Radical Democratic Vision* (Chapel Hill: University of North Carolina Press, 2005); Chris Crass, *Collective Liberation on My Mind* (Montreal: Kersplebedeb, 2001).

13. Chris Dixon, "Against and Beyond: Radical Organizers Building Another Politics in the U.S. and Canada" (PhD diss., University of California at Santa Cruz, 2010).

14. The Midnight Notes and Team Colors collectives usefully remind us that many people who are not politically active in a formal, traditionally recognized way feel the burdens of injustice and carry strong feelings of resentment, prompting them to partake in countless acts of small-scale resistance, such as wasting time while

on the clock at work. See Midnight Notes, "Promissory Notes: From Crisis to Commons," available at http://www.midnight-notes.com; Team Colors Collective, *Wind(s) from Below*, 96.

15. See Nick Dyer-Witheford, *Cyber-Marx: Cycles and Circuits of Struggle in High-Technology Capitalism* (Urbana: University of Illinois, 1999), 62–90.

16. Despite their significant differences with ideas expressed by MNS, the Invisible Committee (*The Coming Insurrection*, 128) admits, "Weapons are a constant in revolutionary situations, but their use is infrequent and rarely decisive at key turning points. . . . When power is in the gutter, it's enough to walk over it." We might usefully conceive of the MNS's theory of change as precisely a theory of "how to put power in the gutter."

17. See Fred Thompson and Jon Bekken, *The Industrial Workers of the World: Its First One Hundred Years, 1905–2005* (Cincinnati: Industrial Workers of the World, 2006).

18. On syndicalism and the IWW, see Schmidt and van der Lucien, *Black Flame*.

19. Michael Hardt and Antonio Negri, *Commonwealth* (Cambridge, MA: Belknap, 2010), 362, 367.

20. Ibid., 369.

21. Despite these moments of agreement, MNS's experiences offer some notes of caution to ideas proposed in *Commonwealth*. For example, Hardt and Negri explain that the strategy of "exodus," which they endorse, "often takes the form of sabotage, withdrawal from collaboration, countercultural practices, and generalized disobedience" (368). As we have seen, MNS veterans caution contemporary activists against the serious pitfalls that exist alongside the benefits of countercultural practices and small-scale forms of withdrawal.

22. On Tolstoy and Gandhi, see David Cortwright, *Gandhi and Beyond: Nonviolence for a New Political Age* (Boulder, CO: Paradigm Publishers, 2009); Joan V. Bondurant, *Conquest of Violence: The Gandhian Philosophy of Conflict* (Princeton, NJ: Princeton University Press, 1958). On de Ligt, see Bart de Ligt, *The Conquest of Violence: An Essay on War and Revolution* (1937; repr., London: Pluto Press, 1989). On Landauer, see Gustav Landauer, *Revolution and Other Writings: A Political Reader*, ed. and trans. Gabriel Kuhn (Oakland, CA: PM Press, 2010).

23. See Andrew Cornell, "A New Anarchism Emerges, 1940–1954," *Journal for the Study of Radicalism* 5, no. 1 (Spring 2011): 105–32; Starhawk, *Webs of Power: Notes from the Global Uprising* (Gabriola Island, BC: New Society Publishers, 2002); David Solnit, ed., *Globalize Liberation: How to Uproot the System and Build a Better World* (San Francisco: City Lights, 2003); Staughton Lynd and Andrej Grubacic, *Wobblies and Zapatistas: Conversations on Anarchism, Marxism, and Radical History* (Oakland, CA: PM Press, 2008).

24. See, for example, David Dellinger, *Revolutionary Nonviolence* (Indianapolis: Bobbs-Merrill, 1970); Barbara Deming, *Revolution and Equilibrium* (New York: Grossman, 1971); Gene Sharp, *Waging Nonviolent Struggle: Twentieth-Century Practice and Twenty-First-Century Potential* (Westford, MA: Porter Sargent, 2005).

25. CR10 Publications Collective, *Abolition Now: Ten Years of Strategy and Struggle Against the Prison-Industrial Complex* (Oakland, CA: AK Press, 2008); INCITE! Women of Color against Violence, *The Color of Violence: The Incite! Anthology* (Boston: South End Press, 2006). On early radical pacifist prison abolitionism, see Liz Samuels, "Improvising on Reality:

The Roots of Prison Abolition," in *The Hidden 1970s: Histories of Radicalism*, ed. Dan Berger (New Brunswick, NJ: Rutgers University Press, 2010), 21–38.

26. For example, Brandon Darby, an organizer-turned-FBI informant and provocateur encouraged two young activists to make Molotov cocktails to be used during protests of the 2008 Republican National Convention, leading to their arrests. See http://theragblog.blogspot.com/2010/03/lisa-fithian-fbi-informant-brandon.html (accessed January 8, 2011).

27. Alex Butterworth, *The World That Never Was: The True Story of Dreamers, Schemers, Anarchists, and Secret Agents* (New York: Pantheon, 2010).

28. Alexandre Skrida, *Facing the Enemy: Anarchist Organization from Proudhon to May 1968*, trans. Paul Sharkey (Oakland, CA: AK Press, 2002); Caroline Cahm, *Kropotkin and the Rise of Revolutionary Anarchism, 1872–1886* (Cambridge: Cambridge University Press, 2002).

29. Sam Dolgoff, interview, WKCR-FM, New York, December 1962, compact disc, Labadie Collection, Harlan Hatcher Graduate Library, University of Michigan, Ann Arbor.

30. Zibechi, *Dispersing Power*; Dussel, *Twenty Theses on Politics*; Benjamin Dangl, *Dancing with Dynamite: Social Movements and States in Latin America* (Oakland, CA: AK Press, 2010); Michael Albert, *The Trajectory of Change* (Boston: South End Press, 2002).

31. Here too, we need to reject simplistic understandings of a prefigurative principle: whether an eight-person affinity group is all white or multiracial is not going to make or break the antiracist character of the revolution. Yet thoughtful efforts to build alliances across racial differences may well contribute to the success or failure of a campaign to prevent a local library or swimming

pool from being closed, or from a group of tenants from being displaced. And these are the sorts of victories that can help us build toward more far-reaching changes.

32. Those currently active in work of this kind, however, strongly recommend establishing systems of accountability, such as advisory boards, to experienced organizers of color. For advising or assistance on creating accountability structures of this sort, see the Catalyst Project, available at http://www.collectiveliberation.org; Training for Change, available at http://www.trainingforchange. org.

33. Betsy Leondar-Wright, "It's Not 'Them,' It's Us!" Class Matters, available at http://www.classmatters.org/2006_07/its-not-them.php (accessed January 8, 2011).

34. For a penetrating consideration of how punk subculture, in particular, can hinder movement building, see Mark Anderson, *All the Power: Revolution without Illusion* (New York: Akashic Books, 2004). I have also written on the subject. See Andy Cornell, "Dear Punk Rock Activism," in *Letters from Young Activists*, ed. Dan Berger, Chesa Boudin, and Kenyon Farrow, 69–75 (New York: Nation Books, 2005). For a defense and celebration of the importance of community and radical cultural initiatives, see Benjamin Shephard, "Play as World-Making: From the Cockettes to the Germs, Gay Liberation to DIY Community Building," in *The Hidden 1970s: Histories of Radicalism*, ed. Dan Berger, 177–94 (New Brunswick, NJ: Rutgers University Press, 2010). Such tensions are intensively examined in Stephen Duncombe, ed., *The Cultural Resistance Reader* (New York: Verso, 2002).

35. See Betsy Leondar-Wright, *Class Matters: Cross-Class Alliance Building for Middle-class Activists* (Gabriola Island, BC:

New Society Publishers, 2005); see also the companion Web site, available at http://www.classmatters.org.

36. See Stevphen Shukaitis, David Graeber, and Erika Biddle, eds., *Constituent Imagination: Militant Investigations, Collective Theorization* (Oakland, CA: AK Press, 2007); Steven Wright, *Storming Heaven: Class Composition and Struggle in Italian Autonomist Marxism* (London: Pluto Press, 2002).

Credits for Anarchist Interventions

Andrew Cornell

Andrew Cornell is an organizer, educator, and writer living in Brooklyn, New York. Originally hailing from Michigan, he first became politically active participating in Food Not Bombs and Anti-Racist Action, learning from the riot grrl movement, and writing and distributing zines. Since then Andrew has been active in antisweatshop, global justice, queer rights, antiwar, and antiprison initiatives. He has worked as a labor organizer, and has supported independent media production by touring with the Bookmobile Project–Projet Mobilivre and working with the *Left Turn* magazine collective. Andrew has taught or cotaught courses on labor history, urban studies, and social theory at universities in New York City, and is currently completing a history of the mid-twentieth-century anarchist movement in the United States. He holds a PhD in American studies from New York University. His writings on capital flight, gay marriage, political strategy, and other topics have appeared in *Clamor*, *MRzine*, *Z Magazine*,

LiP, the *Utne Reader, Critical Moment*, the *Journal for the Study of Radicalism*, and other periodicals and Web sites. He is also a contributor to three books: *Letters from Young Activists* (Nation Books, 2005), *The University against Itself: The NYU Strike and the Future of the Academic Workplace* (Temple University Press, 2008), and *The Hidden 1970s: Histories of Radicalism* (Rutgers University Press, 2010).

Institute for Anarchist Studies

The IAS, a nonprofit foundation established in 1996, aims to support the development of anarchism by creating spaces for independent, politically engaged scholarship that explores social domination and reconstructive visions of a free society. All IAS projects strive to encourage public intellectuals and collective self-reflection within revolutionary and/or movement contexts. To this end, the IAS awards grants twice a year to radical writers and translators worldwide, and has funded some seventy projects over the years by authors from numerous countries, including Argentina, Lebanon, Canada, Chile, Ireland, Nigeria, Germany, South Africa, and the United States. It also publishes the online and print journal *Perspectives on Anarchist Theory*, organizes the Renewing the Anarchist Tradition conference, offers the Mutual Aid Speakers List, and collaborates on this book series, among other projects. The IAS is part of a larger movement seeking to create a nonhierarchical society. It is internally democratic and works in solidarity with people around the globe who share its values. The IAS is completely supported by donations from

anarchists and other antiauthoritarians—like you—and/
or their projects, with any contributions exclusively funding grants and IAS operating expenses; for more information or to contribute to the work of the IAS, see http://
www.anarchist-studies.org/.

AK Press

AK Press is a worker-run collective that publishes
and distributes radical books, visual and audio media, and
other material. We're small: a dozen people who work long
hours for short money, because we believe in what we do.
We're anarchists, which is reflected both in the books we
provide and the way we organize our business. Decisions at
AK Press are made collectively, from what we publish, to
what we distribute and how we structure our labor. All the
work, from sweeping floors to answering phones, is shared.
When the telemarketers call and ask, "who's in charge?" the
answer is: everyone. Our goal isn't profit (although we do
have to pay the rent). Our goal is supplying radical words
and images to as many people as possible. The books and
other media we distribute are published by independent
presses, not the corporate giants. We make them widely
available to help you make positive (or hell, revolutionary)
changes in the world. For more information on AK Press,
or to place an order, see http://www.akpress.org/.

Justseeds Artists' Cooperative

Justseeds Artists' Cooperative is a decentralized community of twenty-two artists who have banded together to

both sell their work, and collaborate with and support each other and social movements. Our Web site is not just a place to shop but also a destination to find out about current events in radical art and culture. We regularly collaborate on exhibitions and group projects as well as produce graphics and culture for social justice movements. We believe in the power of personal expression in concert with collective action to transform society. For more information on Justseeds Artists' Cooperative or to order work, see http://www.justseeds.org/.

Anarchist Interventions Series

Anarchism and Its Aspirations, Cindy Milstein (2010)

Oppose and Propose! Lessons from Movement for a New Society, Andrew Cornell (2011)

Decolonizing Anarchism: An Antiauthoritarian History of India's Liberation Struggle, Maia Ramnath (forthcoming)

Support AK Press!

AK Press is one of the world's largest and most productive anarchist publishing houses. We're entirely worker-run and democratically managed. We operate without a corporate structure—no boss, no managers, no bullshit. We publish close to twenty books every year, and distribute thousands of other titles published by other like-minded independent presses from around the globe.

The Friends of AK program is a way that you can directly contribute to the continued existence of AK Press, and ensure that we're able to keep publishing great books just like this one! Friends pay a minimum of $25 per month, for a minimum three month period, into our publishing account. In return, Friends automatically receive (for the duration of their membership), as they appear, one free copy of every new AK Press title. They're also entitled to a 20% discount on everything featured in the AK Press Distribution catalog and on the website, on any and every order. You or your organization can even sponsor an entire book if you should so choose!

There's great stuff in the works—so sign up now to become a Friend of AK Press, and let the presses roll!

Won't you be our friend? Email friendsofak@akpress.org for more info, or visit the Friends of AK Press website: http://www.akpress.org/programs/friendsofak